ENGLAND
AND THE INTERNATIONAL POLICY
OF THE EUROPEAN GREAT POWERS

1871 – 1914

ENGLAND AND THE INTERNATIONAL POLICY OF THE EUROPEAN GREAT POWERS 1871-1914

Being the Ford Lectures
Delivered to the University of Oxford
in Michaelmas Term, 1929

ALFRED FRANCIS PRIBRAM

FRANK CASS & CO. LTD.
1966

Published by Frank Cass & Co. Ltd.,
10 Woburn Walk, London W.C.1
by arrangement with Oxford University Press

First Edition   1931
New Impression   1966

Printed in Great Britain by
Thomas Nelson (Printers) Ltd., London and Edinburgh.

TO THE MEMORY OF
MY BELOVED WIFE
ELISABETH

PREFACE

IN October, 1929, I was honoured by an invitation to deliver several lectures at Oxford under the title of 'England and the International Policy of the European Great Powers, 1871–1914'. These lectures are here published in their original form as they were delivered.

I have renounced my first intention of expanding them, because they in no sense aim at adding fundamentally to our knowledge of the subject or at bringing forward new explanations of the motives actuating the leading British statesmen. My sole endeavour has been that English scholars should realize how British foreign policy during the years 1871–1914 appears to an unbiassed Continental historian. This motive alone can justify the publication of these lectures: a publication I have only consented to after long hesitation and in response to the repeated solicitations of my English friends.

Since it seems to me unnecessary in a work of this kind to quote all my sources, I have restricted myself to giving an alphabetical list in an Appendix of those of which I have most frequently made use. I desire, however, to draw special attention to one of these sources: the diplomatic documents in the State Archives in Vienna covering the entire period 1871–1914.

I beg leave to draw attention to the fact that instead of the words 'Great Britain' and 'British' the terms 'England' and 'English' have frequently been used as more compatible with the sense in which they are employed by sources and documents other than British.

It is my wish to acknowledge gratefully the help given me in the translation of these lectures into English by some of my younger friends—Ian F. D. Morrow, Dr. Walter Edgar Ives, and Dr. Carleton Sprague Smith.

In conclusion I desire to express my appreciation of the honour conferred upon me by the University of Oxford in inviting me to deliver the Ford Lectures for 1929–30.

A. F. P.

VIENNA,
January 1931.

CONTENTS

INTRODUCTION

THE highest goal of intellectual endeavour—according to Lessing—is the striving for truth, as truth itself is beyond human attainment. In studying the books and documents at my disposal for the purpose of these lectures I constantly strove to keep this goal before my eyes. Yet, this is for no one more difficult than for the student of contemporary history. For he must always be tempted to incorporate into his work those ideas which appeal most to himself or to his hearers or readers. Science, however, is a stern mistress who will not condone the opinions of the day. He who, through weakness or for ulterior reasons, yields to this temptation, breaks faith with her. He who—on the contrary—obeys her commandment must be prepared to face the consequences of pleasing no one. I must leave it to my hearers and readers to decide whether or not I have kept my pledge to strive for truth.

I desire to permit myself two observations by way of introduction to these lectures. The first is concerned with their content; the second with their form. My subject is 'England and the international policy of the European Great Powers, 1871–1914'. That is to say, I shall seek to indicate the policy pursued by leading British statesmen in decisive international questions of their time and to reveal the principles which induced them to act as they did. At the same time it will be my endeavour to sketch the policies of the leading statesmen of the other European Great Powers and to reproduce their opinion of British foreign policy. The fact that I deal first and foremost with the Anglo-German relations is, I trust, justified by the fact that through the use of the monumental German and British publications of diplomatic documents, and through the unreserved access permitted me to the papers in the State Archives in Vienna, I was enabled to follow with exactness the policies pursued by British and German politicians; a degree of exactness that it has not been possible as yet to attain in regard to the relations between the statesmen of the other European Great Powers. A further reason for the prominence given to Anglo-German relations throughout these lectures has been my conviction that these relations were of decisive importance not only for the two countries themselves but also for the fate of Europe and even of the world at large. I should moreover like to point out that I have endeavoured, in so far as the time at my disposal for the delivery of these lectures permitted, to allow the leading statesmen to come forward and speak for themselves. I hope that the adoption of this method will render it easier for my audience to form an independent judgement upon the events touched upon in these lectures.

A word as to the form given to the lectures. I confess that I am very strongly averse to the read lecture and that I am a decided advocate of speaking *ex tempore*, as I always do, and have done throughout my life, when using my mother tongue. For he who listens to a speech should feel that the man standing before him is not only speaking aloud but thinking aloud. And only the right word, born of the inspiration of the moment, will find its way to the heart of the listener. Nevertheless, and not without deep regret, I decided on this occasion to commit my lectures to paper on account of the delicacy of the subject-matter and because I feared I might make mistakes in speech. One word inaptly applied, one ambiguous phrase, could in this special instance give rise to misunderstandings that I desired to avoid at all costs.

LECTURE I
(1871–1879)

SOMEWHERE in his Memoirs Lord Grey of Fallodon makes the trenchant observation that it is a common error of public opinion to think that a statesman, entrusted with the governance of a great empire, concentrates his thoughts unceasingly upon the great objects towards which he is striving to direct the policy of his country. On the contrary, Lord Grey remarks, his greatest happiness for the most part comes from the knowledge that he has finished his labours for the day. But such a statement must not be construed into an admission that a statesman lives solely in and for the day and never raises his eyes from his daily toil to gaze upon the problems that await him on the morrow. Certain fundamental and enduring factors and influences that serve to formulate and condition his policy must be ever present to his mind: otherwise he would never earn for himself the honourable renown of having been a great statesman.

Whoever has studied the actions of responsible British statesmen in their dealings with the Continental Great Powers, from the days when the plan of the English kings to make England a Continental Great Power had perforce to be abandoned, must have become conscious that the actions of one and all of these statesmen have been determined in some measure by the influence of two distinct points of view in regard to what should be the aims to be pursued by British foreign policy. Believers in the first of these two points of view held it to be the predominant aim of British foreign policy to maintain the balance of power between the several Continental Great Powers, or, in other and perhaps better phraseology, the system of counterpoises. For more than four hundred years virtually all British statesmen, without distinction of party or class, have held fast to this belief as the guiding principle of British foreign policy. The existence and influence of this principle in British foreign policy became for the first time clearly discernible during the course of the wars waged in the sixteenth century to defeat the Spanish attempt at world-dominion. During these wars England, under the clever guidance of the Tudors, acted as a kind of indicator in the balance and always at the crucial moment threw her weight into the scale in favour of the declining side. It is noteworthy that time and again the *literati* in England and in France called upon their rulers to cease quarrelling among themselves and to unite against the common enemy. It must also be noted that, even in that age of religious strife, Catholic France and Protestant England made common cause against any enemy who sought to alter the European balance of power in favour of any one nation or any one ruler. Francis Bacon, having in mind the successful issue of the war against Spain, formulated the axiom that any attempt to establish a universal monarchy must be combated from the very moment of its inception. The same principle influenced the policy pursued by English statesmen when France stepped into the position of Spain, and Louis XIV strove, as before him Charles V had done, for domination over Europe. In England the idea of the balance of power gained ground as soon as, after the success of the revolution, the strength of the state began to grow. In a broadsheet of the year 1692 are these words:

'It is to the general interest of the whole of Christendom to bring the House of Austria again into equality with France. This equilibrium is necessary as well for the safety of the peoples as for that of the princes. But it is to the special interest of England to establish again this equality, so that she may again hold the scales in her hand and turn them to whichever side she desires; for this is the one possible role for us, not only that we may continue to be mistress of the sea, but also that we may be capable of deciding the event of war and the terms of peace.'

It was in accordance with this principle that, in alliance with the Emperor and Holland, William III waged war against Louis XIV, and that the English statesmen and generals carried on the war throughout the entire first decade of the eighteenth century. In 1710 it seemed as if France would be beaten to her knees, but England was not willing to allow another Power to take advantage of France's discomfiture and step into her place. She had fought against France on the side of the Habsburgs in the war of the Spanish Succession because she saw in the union of the Spanish and French crowns a menace to the European balance of power, and therefore a menace to herself. This menace was removed by the defeat of the French army, but through the sudden and unexpected death of the Emperor Joseph I, England was confronted by the union of the Spanish and Austrian crowns under a Habsburg. It was in keeping with the foreign policy of England, concentrated as it was on a certain fixed aim, that in this crisis she sought to sever herself from her allies and to come to an agreement with her late enemy, whose friendship she now regarded as necessary for the preservation of the balance of power.

The same principle animated England in her wars with Napoleon I and Nicholas I. Always her object in going to war was the same—to prevent any single Continental Power from attaining to such a position of superiority as might endanger the balance of power among the Continental Great Powers.

The second great principle underlying British foreign policy was no less permanent in character. From the moment when the loss of Calais bereft England of her last foothold on the other side of the Channel, it became the lasting concern of British statesmen to prevent Belgium from passing into the permanent possession of the strongest Continental Power. For it was from here that the greatest danger could threaten the island kingdom whose strongest defence was the sea. This consideration exercised a decisive influence upon England's wars against Philip II and Louis XIV, and it is also noteworthy that England first determined to intervene in the struggle against the French Revolution at the moment when the French army occupied Belgium. The extent to which this Belgian question influenced British statesmen throughout the whole course of the nineteenth century is revealed by their conduct at the Congress of Vienna. At that Congress the British representatives insisted with courageous pertinacity upon the union of Holland with Belgium in order to erect still a stronger barrier against expansionist desires in France. Later the influence of this question is revealed in their opposition to the attempts of France to gain the Belgian throne for a French prince at a time when it had become apparent that a continuance of the union of the two kingdoms, Holland and Belgium, was a practical impossibility. No State has ever intervened more strenuously in defence of the neutrality of Belgium than has England, and it is unquestionable that rumours of Napoleon III's plans for the annexation of Belgium brought about a change of attitude towards that monarch on the part of British statesmen in the latter years of his reign.

France was at that time leading among the European Powers. Her further expansion was of necessity dangerous to the peace of Europe and to the system of the balance of power, the upholding of which was the lasting concern of England. This danger was overcome through the victory of German arms in the Franco-German war—a war which closed one epoch in European history and opened another. On the battlefields of France the German people realized their long-cherished dream of unity; the old German Empire arose once more in a new form and with new frontiers, yet in all its former brilliance. In the place formerly occupied among the Great Powers by Prussia there now stood Imperial Germany with even greater prestige than was formerly enjoyed by Prussia.

England, indeed, took no part in the war: an attitude dictated to her alike by her interests and the aversion to war of her leading statesmen of that day. Nevertheless the Government, and still more public opinion, viewed the unification of Germany with friendly eyes. Many people shared in the opinion expressed by Lord A. Loftus, the British ambassador at Berlin, when, writing directly after the battle of Königgrätz, he said that the appearance of a new Central European Great Power accorded with British interests: 'for a strong Germany would look to England for moral support and would need an alliance with a great sea-power.' The neutrality of England during the Franco-German war was of untold value to Bismarck, since, in conjunction with the neutrality of Russia in his rear, it alone enabled him to bring the war with France to a victorious end without arousing a European conflagration. But with the unexpectedly brilliant triumph of German arms an anti-Prussian feeling began to manifest itself in British public opinion and among British statesmen. This was justified by the fact that it became apparent that Bismarck laid greater weight on the fulfilment of Russian desires than of those of England.

At the end of October, 1870, while the Franco-German war was still in progress, Prince Gortschakoff, the leader of foreign policy in Russia, had made known to the signatories to the peace of 1856 that the Tsar no longer held himself bound by the stipulation, so oppressive to Russia, prohibiting her from retaining war-ships in the Black Sea. Gortschakoff's memorandum caused much surprise and indignation in England, where the traditional policy of opposition to Russia was still in force. Granville declared that no single power could free itself from any of the stipulations of a treaty except by obtaining the previous consent of the co-signatories. 'What Gortschakoff has done', he said, 'is to bring the entire authority and efficacy of treaties under the discretionary control of each one of the powers who may have signed them, the result of which would be the entire destruction of treaties in their essence.' It was the same argument as that with which England opposed later the Treaty of San Stefano in 1878, and the annexation of Bosnia-Herzegovina in 1908. England demanded a conference. It met in London, but the course of its deliberations did not proceed entirely in accordance with the wishes of England; for the wishes of Russia were satisfied in one essential point. The Paris prohibition concerning the Black Sea was removed, and while the Straits of the Bosphorus and Dardanelles remained closed to Russian men-of-war, they were opened to the passage of Russian merchantmen. In order to comprehend the importance of this event, which clearly demonstrated to the British the high value Bismarck placed upon good relations with Russia and how little he was prepared to sacrifice those good relations to the desires of England, it is necessary to remember that the Near Eastern question now began to be one of the most important factors in the politics of the Great Powers in Europe; the more so, as a concerted world policy in the seventies can be spoken of only with extreme caution. Extra-European questions were indeed already influencing the progress of international politics in Europe, but they were yet far from drawing all, or almost all, the Great Powers within their orbit. Their influence was the more noticeable, however, in that the international antagonism still predominating in Anglo-Russian politics had spread from Central Asia to the Near East.

European policy in the Near East was not less influenced by the looming of the Egyptian question. But European questions still had preponderance over extra-European ones during the seventies since the two extra-European Great Powers of the future, the United States of America and Japan, were so occupied with their own political difficulties that they could not actively participate in European questions.

If Bismarck's policy in the London Conference earned for him the dislike of the British ministers, their anxiety only deepened when the harsh terms of the Peace of Frankfort were made public. While a weakening of France would have been approved, it was quite another thing for another power to achieve the hegemony of Europe in her place. Morley at once declared that 'Europe has lost a mistress and gained a master', while Disraeli gave voice to his fear that the balance of power was completely destroyed and that England suffered more than the others through the change. Bismarck, for his part, sought to maintain friendly relations with England, and he would gladly have entered into an alliance with her—an alliance that would have guaranteed to him the advantages gained in the Peace of Frankfort and the isolation of France. This, however, was not in the interests of England so long as she could not hope for the support of Germany in her rivalry with Russia. And what took place in the next few years only served to strengthen the fears voiced by Disraeli.

It was not only gratitude for the services rendered by Russia in the Franco-German war which decided the policy of Bismarck. What actuated him to be of service to Russia was, more than anything else, the desire to isolate France, to avert an alliance between France, Austria-Hungary, and Russia. It was eminently characteristic of Bismarck's train of thought that he should see in Germany's partnership in an alliance, strong enough to set any number of foes at defiance, the best way for her to avoid all danger of hostilities. He thought this security guaranteed to Germany when he successfully brought about a confederation between those three Eastern European Great Powers who had once joined in the Holy Alliance. The union of the old allies which he achieved in 1872 and 1873 in the new Entente of the Three Emperors gave him the greatest satisfaction. But questions of international politics, chief among them the prevention of the formation of a coalition dangerous to Germany's future, were not the only problems Bismarck was called upon to weigh. There was also the problem of the ever-increasing danger to the conservative monarchical Powers constituted by the socialist International, a movement which at that time had newly come into existence, a social revolutionary change which influenced Bismarck and the rulers of the three Eastern Powers to a far higher degree than was realized until recently. Through the publication by the German Government of the documents in their archives, and through the unreserved throwing open of the State Archives in Vienna, it is possible to examine the motives underlying the transactions of the historic personages of these states. For the first time it can be proved that this common danger acted as one of the closest bonds between the rulers of Austria-Hungary, Russia, and Germany.

Bismarck wished to gain England also as an ally in the fight against this new common enemy. Already, in the middle of June, 1871, he had entered into correspondence with Granville regarding an understanding as to 'common defence against the common enemy' and as to the 'moral responsibility of England as the native land of the "International" '. But his suggestion met with no acceptance at the hands of the British Government, and Gladstone took a decided stand in defence of the right of asylum and English freedom. The conservatism of the three Empires was irreconcilable with British liberalism. In this sense the Triple Entente of 1873 revealed the widening of the gulf between England and the Eastern European Great Powers, although Bismarck opposed the attempt of Russia to use the alliance as a weapon against England and refused to approve the military convention between Russia and Germany which was concluded without his consent. Nevertheless, and despite all Bismarck's endeavours to accommodate England in all matters in which German interests were not directly involved, the relations between the two countries remained strained.

The rapid development of the German Empire was watched with increasing anxiety in England, and as early as 1872 Odo Russell observed: 'Napoleon III was not more powerful than Bismarck is in this moment.' The centre of power and of diplomacy had unquestionably been transferred to Berlin. Rumours that Bismarck planned the inclusion of Holland and Belgium in the German Empire found credence in many quarters in England. Disraeli, who directed British foreign policy from 1874 and who was animated with the desire to secure for his country once again a decisive voice in European affairs, watched with anxiety the ever-growing influence of Germany under Bismarck's leadership. When in the spring of 1875 military circles in Berlin, alarmed by the rapid recovery of France and her increasing armaments, began to speak of a preventive war, and when a newspaper in close touch with the German Government published an article under the heading 'War in Sight', excitement in London rose to fever-pitch. The article in question, as we now know, was not inspired by Bismarck, although he approved of it as a warning to France. In concert with Russia, Disraeli determined to protest to Berlin—a protest that met with a conciliatory reply from Bismarck calculated to allay public anxiety. But Bismarck was quick to perceive from this action on the part of England and Russia that neither power would with complacency witness the further weakening of France. Any such intention was indeed far from Bismarck's mind. His plans were made with a view to retain for Germany that which she had gained, and to prevent France from allying herself with England and Russia in the hope of thereby regaining through a successful war her lost territories, and the commanding position she had occupied in the councils of Europe before 1870. These were the considerations that induced Bismarck, despite his personal dislike of Gortschakoff, to avoid a breach with Russia, and at the same time to seek to restore friendly relations between Germany and England. His first attempt in this latter direction met with success. Lord Derby declared at the end of July, 1875, that no divergency of interests separated England and Germany: he hoped that good relations would soon be re-established and that the passage of time would only serve to intensify them.

Bismarck then took a further step, and towards the end of the year his 'confidant', Bucher, appeared in London. To the present day mystery envelops Bucher's mission. That Bismarck, as a German historian would have us believe, wanted to assure himself of England's support for the carrying out of a policy of colonial and economic expansion is hardly credible. What is more probable is that he wanted to find out what attitude England would adopt towards the conflict that had arisen a short time before in the Balkans. Bismarck—as we know to-day—employed all his energy to bring about a peaceful compromise between the three Powers (England, Russia, and Austria-Hungary) having the greatest interests at stake in the Balkans. It was with this object in view that he brought forward in London at the beginning of 1876 his plan of compensations, a plan that was rejected by the British Cabinet. In rejecting this plan the Cabinet were actuated by their desire to maintain the territorial integrity of Turkey and by their fear lest Bismarck's proposed solution, which was likely to be injurious to England's position in Egypt, might be the cause of new dangers. The Berlin Memorandum of May, 1876, met with an equally cold reception in London. When, however, the danger of a Russo-Turkish war grew daily more imminent, British statesmen began to think of an alliance both with Austria-Hungary, whose interests, in so far as they involved rivalry with Russia, were parallel with those of England, and with Germany. This is not the place in which to trace the course of the negotiations which followed upon the decision of the British Cabinet to seek an alliance with the Central Empires. To-day we know that from the autumn of 1876 onwards secret negotiations took place between London and Vienna with a view to securing united procedure in regard to the Near Eastern Question. I might add that in the State Archives in Vienna there exist as yet unpublished secret documents which go to prove that drafts of a treaty were drawn up by both parties. But mutual distrust caused the failure of the negotiations. The Viennese Government feared that England might seek to throw the heaviest burden of a war with Russia on the shoulders of the Danubian Monarchy, whilst in England suspicions were entertained of Andrassy, whose prolonged negotiations with Russia had become known to the British Cabinet. The attempt of the British Government to induce Germany to take decisive steps against Russia met with no greater success.

As Bismarck often said, Germany was not prepared to pull the chestnuts out of the fire for England. But if Bismarck refused to sacrifice Austria-Hungary at the instance of Russia in September, 1876, he was in consequence all the more willing to meet Russia in purely Oriental questions to the utmost of his ability. What he most decidedly refused to do was to use his influence at St. Petersburg on behalf of British policy in the East. Above all, his endeavours were directed, as always, to prevent the outbreak of a war that must endanger the peace of Europe. For this purpose he initiated the negotiations with England in the last months of 1876 and the early days of 1877. But while he desired an understanding with England, he had no intention of replacing one alliance with another. What he most of all sought to bring about was an understanding between England and Russia, an understanding which, however, would not prevent these two Powers from continuing in a rivalry welcome to Germany. 'If England and Russia', he declared in June, 1877, 'were to come to an understanding on the basis of the possession of Egypt for the former and the Black Sea for the latter, both would have an interest in the maintenance of the *status quo* for a long time. Yet both would be brought, as regards their greatest interests, into a rivalry which would render it very unlikely that they would both be members at the same time of a coalition directed against us.' As is very clearly to be seen, Bismarck desired no definite alliance with England, but rather the creation of a general international situation favourable to German interests. The fact that on the outbreak of the Russo-Turkish war British statesmen believed themselves to be called upon actively to defend British interests was most welcome to Bismarck. It is true that they would not hear of active participation in the war so long as this could be by any means avoided—what they demanded was the maintenance of freedom of communication between Europe and the East by means of the Suez Canal, the exclusion of Egypt from the sphere of military operations, and the recognition by Russia of the inviolability of Constantinople and the Straits. They entered into a verbal understanding with Austria-Hungary—July 26, 1877—affirming solidarity of interests, and pledging the two governments to identical but separate diplomatic action and, if necessary, to subsequent united military measures.

The Russo-Turkish war lasted longer than had been anticipated, and ended in victory for Russia only after the Rumanian ruler, at the head of his army, had joined forces with her. In March, 1878, the Peace of San Stefano was signed, by which Russia, disregarding her agreements with Austria-Hungary at Reichstadt and Schönbrunn, divided the spoils between herself and Bulgaria, whom she intended to make her vassal. Bosnia and Herzegovina were declared autonomous, a declaration which was a direct challenge to the Government in Vienna in view of the agreements of 1876 and 1877. Andrassy thereupon, in February, 1878, called upon the European Great Powers for aid. In this course he had the support of England, where since the beginning of the year 1878 a large majority of the nation had given expression to its dislike of Russia and its desire for war. Opinion within the Cabinet was divided. Some ministers were outspokenly hostile to Russia; others—among them Lord Derby—were resolutely opposed to a war; others again, while not excluding the possibility of war, did not wish to embark immediately upon armed intervention. How far Lord Beaconsfield, who was regarded by the nation as a supporter of an active policy, was in earnest in threatening Russia, or whether he hoped thereby to compel the Russian Government to make concessions that would enable him to secure for the 'bellicose' Queen a bloodless victory, it is not for me to determine. What is certain is that, ably supported by Salisbury, who had succeeded Derby at the Foreign Office, Beaconsfield gained his end without involving England in a war. This achievement of Beaconsfield and Salisbury will be looked upon as a masterpiece of diplomacy for all time; more especially the manner in which they contrived to secure Russian acceptance of their principal demands, the consent of Turkey to an English occupation of Cyprus, and the consent of Austria-Hungary to enter into an agreement with England of real value for the latter's interests: 'All this by means of treaties, each concluded separately with the interested Power, and of the existence of which the other non-signatory but interested Powers were unaware at the opening of the Congress of Berlin on June 13, 1878.'

Supported by these treaties, the British representatives could witness without anxiety the proceedings of the

Congress at Berlin. With great truth Dr. Gooch writes. 'The peace of honour, which Beaconsfield on his return announced at Charing Cross to an admiring crowd, had virtually been secured at Downing Street before the beginning of the Congress.' The collaboration of Beaconsfield and Salisbury with Bismarck in Berlin lessened the mistrust with which the British statesmen had followed the policy of the Imperial Chancellor. But I beg leave to doubt whether, as is often stated, Bismarck at that time put forward a direct request for an alliance in his conversations with Beaconsfield. At the same time the disappointment which he saw written upon the faces of the Russian delegates at the outcome of the Congress made it desirable for Bismarck to come to some understanding with Beaconsfield in quite an unbinding form, as to the possibility of common action in the event of certain emergencies arising. But he was at that time not inclined to adopt a definitely anti-Russian policy at the desire of England, even though by doing so he could have obtained from England adequate compensation.

There is no doubt but that the conclusions of the Congress of Berlin meant a heavy defeat for Russia. She had to cede a large part of what she had gained by the Peace of San Stefano. The most important fact for international politics, however, was that the breach then opened between Russia and Germany was never again completely closed. For in many and influential anti-German circles in St. Petersburg, the conviction prevailed that Bismarck had betrayed Russia. Alexander II described the proceedings of the Congress as a European coalition led against Russia by Prince Bismarck. Neither England nor Austria-Hungary, the chief enemies of Russia, but rather Germany's leading statesman was looked upon in Russia as the man most responsible for her humiliation. Bismarck emphasized, and emphasized with truth, the fact that he had spared no physical or mental effort to further the cause of his great neighbour. But the Russian press grew ever more antagonistic to Germany, and the anti-German statesmen at the court of St. Petersburg, Ignatiev and Miljutin, ever more powerful. Moreover, Bismarck was forced to recognize that Alexander II was identifying himself more and more with the Pan-Slav party, and that Russia was adopting an increasingly menacing attitude. In the summer of 1879, Alexander said to the German ambassador: 'If you desire to continue the friendship which has united us for a hundred years, you must alter your bearing towards Russia; if you do not, this matter will not end well.' At the same time it came to be known in Berlin that Russian troops had been stationed on the Prussian frontier, and, soon after that, a dispatch full of complaints of the conduct of the German Government, and especially of that of Bismarck, was handed to Emperor William. We know how often and how powerfully Bismarck was haunted by the *cauchemar des alliances*, and how frequently he warned his Imperial Master of the danger of an alliance between Russia, France, and Austria-Hungary—an alliance, the conclusion of which at this particular moment he feared from the information contained in the dispatches he received. From the documents now available to us we learn that anxiety lest a change should come about in Austria's foreign policy—an anxiety that increased in proportion as the internal state of Austria gave cause for fear that a Slavophil policy would be inaugurated—was one of the fundamental and decisive motives that induced Bismarck to prosecute so actively his attempt to conclude an alliance with the Danubian Monarchy. There is no need in this connexion to narrate the progress of events in detail. We know how Andrassy, Bismarck's opponent in this diplomatic struggle, succeeded in gaining Bismarck's signature to a treaty directed solely against Russia and not—as Bismarck originally desired—against every enemy. We are also aware that this treaty, signed

October 7, 1879, was of a purely defensive nature. Finally, we have learnt how unusually difficult it was for Bismarck to gain the consent of his aged sovereign to this treaty—a consent only obtained after a tremendous struggle between the two men and the most determined resistance on the part of the Emperor—and then only under certain conditions. In his conflict with the Emperor Bismarck repeatedly emphasized England's interests and their importance for the Central Powers. As early as in his dispatch of August 17, 1879, in which he gave expression to his apprehension lest Russia should ally herself with France and Austria-Hungary in war against Germany, Bismarck suggested urgently not only a union with the Danubian Monarchy but also a good understanding with England. On September 1 he specified as one of the grounds for an alliance with Austria-Hungary the fact that 'she will carry England along with her'. And he added: 'The two Western Powers and Austria are absolutely and without exception against Russia in all questions relating to the Near East, and I am convinced that on account of this Austria and France are already bound by promises made to England.'

It is necessary to bear in mind these reflections of Bismarck's to obtain a right understanding of the negotiations that took place in England towards the end of September, 1879. About the middle of that month Bismarck determined to concede Andrassy's demands, and drew up a draft of a treaty directed against Russia. He was resolutely determined to strain every nerve to win over his Emperor to assent to a German-Austrian treaty drafted in accordance with Andrassy's wishes. For this purpose he addressed appeal after appeal to Emperor William I. But the Emperor would not hear of a treaty that was directed against Russia, and Bismarck was forced to reckon with the possibility that he would fail to win the Emperor's consent. Hence it was very natural that he should wish to learn to what extent he could reckon upon English support alongside, or in place of that of Austria-Hungary, in the event of a war between Germany and Russia. Bismarck therefore instructed Count Münster, the German ambassador at London, to sound the British Government in this sense. It was fully in accord with Bismarck's ideas of the manner in which negotiations must be carried on with England that he ordered Münster to say in London: 'It is hardly necessary to state that there are no direct German interests involved to restrain us from fulfilling Russia's desires to have our support for her policy in the East. It would only be the great value we should place upon our friendship with Austria-Hungary and Great Britain that would induce us to refuse our support to Russia in this matter. But before we embark upon such a policy we must know what we can expect from England in event of our thereby involving ourselves in disputes with our Eastern neighbour.' Münster's account of his conversation on this matter with Beaconsfield on September 26 differs in important points from that given by Beaconsfield, in his report to Queen Victoria. According to Beaconsfield, Münster proposed a general alliance between Germany, Austria, and Great Britain. To this proposal Beaconsfield replied that, while he was at all times personally ready to come to an understanding with Germany, the English people would not be prepared to assent to any action on the part of England capable of being interpreted as an act of hostility to France, as the economic, social, and to a certain extent political relations of the two states were very intimate. Münster, however, reported to Berlin that Beaconsfield had described Germany and Austria as the natural allies of England, and that he had declared he would gladly enter into an alliance with Germany. 'If we come to an agreement between us', Beaconsfield had said, so Münster relates, 'I see the peace of Europe assured for a long time. If the Prince will help us in the East, where our interests go hand

in hand with Austria's, we will undertake, in the event of
this policy bringing Russia into conflict with Germany,
that France will not be able to move. We will in that case
keep France quiet. You may depend on us.' Direct active
assistance to Germany in event of a war with Russia,
Beaconsfield—as we see—did not promise; and that was
the very thing that Bismarck desired. For England to keep
an observant eye upon France was not sufficient for Bismarck. Thus this attempt to bring about an Anglo-German
alliance failed. If it had succeeded, a different direction
would have been given to the course of events in international politics.

In order to be able to judge rightly the attitude of English
statesmen to these negotiations, it is necessary to take into
consideration the situation in which England then found
herself.

In Central Asia the Russians were advancing steadily
from the direction of Bokhara and Khiva towards Merv
(1878). Then came disputes over Kabul with Russia,
whilst in the Transvaal trouble was threatening and the
Zulus were in rebellion. And although England at that
time worked hand in hand with France in Egypt, she could
not afford to allow France a free hand there. England
wished to avoid hurting France's feeling for fear lest she
might lend an ear to Russian overtures for an alliance.
Here again one can see the difficulties barring the way to
a German-English alliance. England wished to keep the
Central Powers apart from Russia, and to assure herself
of the armed assistance of Germany in event of a war with
Russia; but she refused to promise similar support to
Germany in event of a Franco-German war. Bismarck,
however, demanded a definite promise of active participation on the part of England in event of a war between
France and Germany; a promise that seemed to him
doubly necessary seeing that he could not, in accordance
with the conditions laid down in the draft-treaty with

Austria, reckon upon the armed assistance of the latter. England's attempt to isolate Russia without incurring the enmity of France, and Bismarck's desire to complete the isolation of France without embroiling himself with Russia, were incompatible and irreconcilable. When in the first half of October, 1879, British statesmen, like Beaconsfield and Salisbury, showed themselves ready to go further in making concessions to Germany by holding out the prospect of England's active intervention in any conflict between Russia and either of the Central Powers, the alliance between Germany and Austria was already an accomplished fact; and Bismarck felt that he could dispense with England's help. Moreover Saburow—the Russian ambassador—appeared in Berlin with proposals that seemed to Bismarck to hold out the promise of the establishment of good relations with Russia: a promise that he was all the more desirous of seeing fulfilled in that he had just experienced the reluctance of the aged Emperor to permit Germany to be involved in an anti-Russian policy. The negative outcome of the negotiations with England, when viewed from the standpoint of our present knowledge of all that has happened since that day, may be deemed to have been a misfortune both for the peace of the world and for Germany in particular. At that time, however, it was not so regarded by either side. Beaconsfield, indeed, wrote to the Queen: 'Your Majesty is as free as air, and that too without showing any want of sympathy with the Austro-German view.' Bismarck, for his part, thought that the interests of the German Empire had been safeguarded, and he was resolved to make his future relations with England depend upon the course of events.

LECTURE II

AFTER the settlement of the Near Eastern crisis, and the conclusion of the German-Austro-Hungarian alliance, international relations in Europe became less strained; not only because the question of the Near East, at least for some years, provided fewer centres of friction than it had in the past, or, for that matter, would in the future; but also because now, for the first time since 1870, extra-European politics became conspicuous within the fabric of world politics. Though fresh possibilities of friction were brought into existence by the shifting of the political centre of gravity (especially with reference to colonial expansion), these possibilities served, at least at first, to assure European peace. Russia extended her power in Asia; England enlarged her possessions in practically every part of the world, and became ruler of Egypt; and the French Republic zealously tried to find compensation for its European losses in founding colonies. The newly-formed Great Powers, Germany and Italy, as well as Belgium, were added to the list of powers in pursuit of colonies. That these occupations were not so detrimental to the peace of Europe as might have been expected, was partly due to the fact that Bismarck not merely approved of such efforts, especially on the part of France, but in a certain sense furthered them. He did this in order to divert the interest of the French Republic from its position in Europe. But, at the same time, he realized that it was impossible to hope that France would become reconciled to the loss of Alsace-Lorraine and of her position as leading European Great Power. The circumvention of the danger which threatened Germany and the peace of Europe from this attitude, was, according to his often-expressed conviction, to be obtained in one way only: so to isolate France in Europe that she could not hope to engage in a war of revenge with any prospect of success. Because of this conviction, Bismarck had concluded the alliance with Austria-Hungary, and now for the same reason he was at pains to strengthen that alliance by the inclusion in it of other European Powers. One addition, as the result of the general political situation arising from the Congress of Berlin, might have been Great Britain. Andrassy, the Austro-Hungarian minister for Foreign Affairs, thought that this Power, directly interested as she was in the consolidation of Central Europe, might be a possible support for Austria-Hungary; and in the course of his negotiations with Bismarck, he had proposed England's entry into the German-Austro-Hungarian alliance. We have seen Bismarck's attitude to this idea and we have seen how, after the conclusion of the alliance with Austria and the *rapprochement* with Russia, he would no longer listen to any proposal for the inclusion of England within the Dual Alliance, fearing that Germany might thus be involved in the British-Russian controversy in the Near East. But the Viennese statesmen held with equal firmness to their desires. Haymerle, Andrassy's successor, favoured the scheme. For years he had been Austrian ambassador at Rome, and he feared that, in the event of a war between Austria and Russia, Italy might participate as the opponent of the former. 'Russia', he said at the end of 1879, 'is our arch-enemy. Our policy in Berlin agrees entirely with that of England. The enlistment of England's interests would mean security for us against our southern neighbour Italy, who would never think of attacking an Austria-Hungary allied to England.' He alluded to the fact that, with Bismarck's approval, he had imparted to the British Government as early as the autumn of 1879 the fundamental idea of the German-Austrian alliance. This information had been well received in London, Salisbury expressing the opinion that this was one of the best things that could have happened for the whole world. For at that time it was still one of the principles of English policy that there should be a Central Europe strong enough to stem the tide of pan-Slavism. In February, 1880, the Vienna Government addressed the following question to Berlin: 'Whether, and to what extent, we should further enlighten Beaconsfield and Salisbury in order to obtain promises or declarations pledging England, in case of a conflict with Russia, or an indirect collision with her which might threaten our position in the Orient, to use her influence, her direct pressure, or, should occasion arise, a naval demonstration to prevent Italy from attacking us and to safeguard the Adriatic for us.'

Negotiations carried on in London in March served to reveal that England was prepared in this sense to defend Austro-Hungarian interests. Salisbury declared that in reply to an inquiry of the Italian Government in the previous year Beaconsfield had stated that the conclusion of an alliance between Russia and Italy would be regarded by England as a *casus belli*. The British statesmen also showed a disposition at that time to enter into the Dual Alliance with the stipulation that any resumption of relations with Russia, as advocated by Bismarck, should be directed solely to the end of preventing conflicts with Russia. The Viennese Government was quite aware that it would be no easy task to win over Germany to some sort of Triple Alliance directed against Russia. It believed that William I would not give such a project his consent. It declared, therefore, its willingness, in case Bismarck should approve and hold out hopes of his support, to enlist England's aid merely for Austria-Hungary. This suggestion for securing England's co-operation did not find favour with Bismarck. He declared that England's co-operation was neither advisable nor necessary. Should there be a conflict between the Central Powers and Russia, England, he believed, would in any case hold Italy in check. Moreover, he was afraid of giving Russia fresh ground for alarm through the bugbear of a coalition, and of nullifying the efforts of those Russian statesmen who wished for friendship with the Central Great Powers. This, above all, Bismarck was anxious to avoid; for he still considered the reconciliation of the Cabinets of Vienna and Petersburg to be the chief goal first and last. He therefore decided not to request direct assistance from the British Government, for he feared that England's entry into the Central European alliance would compel Germany's acquiescence in a policy which he thought contrary to her interests. He was, however, then as always, ready to be on good terms with England, and to negotiate for her closer connexion with the Central Great Powers. But nothing came of these negotiations, and when in the spring of 1880 there was a change of government in England, the Liberals, led by Gladstone, believing that Beaconsfield had played too much into Bismarck's hand, and wishing to avoid war with Russia as well as to leave open a way of approach to France with regard to the Egyptian situation, had no inclination to join the Central Powers.

Gladstone preferred to retain a free hand and to overcome the imminent danger by a reserved attitude in foreign policy. He withdrew the English legation from Kabul; under pressure of the Boer revolt gave a measure of partial freedom to the Transvaal; and endeavoured to pursue a joint policy with France in Egypt. Furthermore it is clear that by reason of their utterly different political ideas no less than their differing personalities, friendly relations were impossible between Bismarck and Gladstone. At the same time, in my opinion, it is a mistake to attach any special significance to the change of government in England in regard to British foreign policy. Often against his will, and very tardily, Gladstone was compelled to pursue Beaconsfield's imperialistic policy. On the other hand, Bismarck, despite his reserved attitude in the question of the incorporation of England into the Dual

Alliance, as also in the Eastern Question (at that time England was the protagonist of Greece in the Turko-Greek dispute and sought in vain for the active support of Germany), remained true to his desire to maintain good relations with England. He did not, however, run the risk of having his plans upset through paying too great regard to British interests. What he wished was to win back Russia and to re-establish the old League of the Three Emperors.

The coolness which entered into the relations between the Cabinets of Vienna and London in consequence of Gladstone's strong anti-Austrian attitude helped to overcome the dislike that was felt in Vienna for an alliance with Russia. Austrian statesmen justly saw in Russia the most dangerous rival to Austria's policy of seeking to extend her sphere of influence towards the South-East, the only direction in which such an attempt appeared likely to be crowned with success. But it seems to me necessary to point out here that it was not only the requirements of foreign policy which influenced Bismarck's attitude. One of the principal reasons for carrying out his designs lay in the fact that it was to the interests of the monarchical states and dynasties to protect themselves by this alliance against the growth and increase of democratic and anti-monarchical forces. Again and again Bismarck had urged the importance of this fact upon the Cabinets of St. Petersburg and Vienna. At the moment when he had succeeded in winning over Russia, but was still meeting with opposition in Vienna, Bismarck induced his sovereign, in January, 1881, to write a holograph letter to Francis Joseph in which he said:

'In an agreement between the three Emperors I perceive not only actual and valuable promises, but also a great moral weight to balance European peace and monarchical policy in the scale against those movements which have shattered Western Europe, and which may carry the republican principle beyond

the frontiers of France into our midst. The moral weight of
the three great monarchies, as long as they remain united, is
sufficient to assure their own security—and perhaps even that
of the rest of Europe—against the menace of anarchy.'

Bismarck attained his object. On June 18, 1881, the
treaty was signed. This treaty achieved a temporary compromise between the interests of Russia and Austria in the
Balkans, but at the same time marked—what for our
purpose is of importance—an estrangement from England.
For Bismarck hoped through this treaty to be the first to
break away from the dogma that the possession of Constantinople by Russia would be an international danger—
an opinion at that time strongly held by England. 'I consider', he said in effect, 'these ideas to be unfounded, and
I fail to see why a British interest should be raised to the
dignity of a European interest.'

At the time when the league of the three Emperors was
signed, negotiations were in progress which aimed at the
inclusion of Italy within the system of the Central European alliances. The path of these negotiations was strewn
with difficulties, but Bismarck's inexhaustible patience
carried his diplomacy to victory by successfully surmount-
ing them all. On May 20, 1882, the first Triple Alliance
was signed. The purposes of this treaty were explicitly
defensive in every respect. It was intended to secure the
allied sovereigns and their states against any disturbance
of the peace from without or within. The significance
attached to the treaty as a safeguard for the monarchical
principle and a protection against destructive social movements should not be forgotten.

By the conclusion of this Triple Alliance, co-existent
with, but independent of the German-Austro-Hungarian
alliance of October, 1879, and by the League of the Three
Emperors of 1881, Bismarck had considerablystrengthened
the ramparts which he had raised against aggression on
the part of France. An additional source of strength was

the fact that England, who had been made aware of the particular object of the Triple Alliance, welcomed its conclusion. Italy would have liked to go further, for her statesmen pointed out that it was a necessity for Italy to maintain amicable relations with the strongest sea-power, to whose fleet Italy's long coast-line offered an easy object of attack. Italy, therefore, proposed the signature of a secret protocol by which the door would be left open for England either to come into the alliance as a whole or to assent to those articles which laid down mutual neutrality in event of war. This proposal fell short of acceptance both in Vienna and Berlin. Gladstone's sharp words against Austria in his election speech in 1880 had offended the Cabinet of Vienna, while Bismarck showed little inclination to sponsor the entry of England into the Triple Alliance, because he feared that the alliance would in that case gain a distinctly anti-Russian character.

But, on the other hand, out of regard for the geographical situation of Italy, which compelled her to pay particular regard to England, Bismarck lent his support to the desire of the Italian Government to see it clearly stated in an additional clause that the treaty was in no case to be regarded as directed against England. Bismarck himself looked upon this declaration as unnecessary. 'The idea', he said, 'of declaring war upon England is entirely foreign to each of the contracting parties—none of whom could wage it with success. But if England declares war, there is no choice.'

Whether or not England was at that time prepared to accept an invitation to join in the Triple Alliance is a question I prefer not to answer. When we remember Gladstone's distrust of Bismarck, and the dislike of British politicians on principle to conclude secret alliances, it is at least open to doubt. Yet it is unquestionable that the tension between Russia and England in Asia, and the rivalry with France in Egypt, after the hostile reception in

England accorded to the Tunis Incident, seemed to counsel the advisability of the British Government's establishing as friendly relations as possible with the Central Powers. The withdrawal of France from the Egyptian Question brought about by Freycinet, Gambetta's successor, rendered it necessary for the British Government, despite the dislike of the liberals to such a policy, to prosecute the struggle with the anti-British movement in Egypt. This policy of repression led to the bombardment of Alexandria and the occupation of Egypt. While this certainly denoted an increase of British power, it also involved England in conflicts of which the outcome could not be foreseen. It is conceivable that in these circumstances the desire for a closer relationship with the Central Powers increased among influential circles in England. What is certain is that at the beginning of September, 1882, the German Crown Prince, acting under the influence of his wife, the English Princess Victoria, and with the knowledge of his brother-in-law, the Prince of Wales, sent Bismarck a most interesting memorandum in which he stated that he had received the impression 'that in England a sufficiently high value was set upon an alliance with Germany and Austria for such an alliance to be given a far-reaching interpretation in the sense of making common cause against every danger threatening peace'. It is very questionable whether Gladstone and Granville approved this step. It did not correspond with their ideas, nor could they have considered it to hold forth much prospect of success. If that be so, the answer returned by Bismarck justified them. The answer was, in effect, a carefully worded refusal.

'In consequence of the want of direct German interest in the future of Egypt'—so it ran—'and because of the certainty that we shall have to reckon with France, no less than the possibility that we shall have to reckon with Russia, as enemies, I have represented to His Majesty the necessity, irrespectively of the present British Government and their sometimes extraordinary policy, of avoiding every conflict with the British nation and public opinion in England that could arouse British national feeling against us, unless we are compelled to do so through overwhelming German interests.'

But Bismarck added that it was not Germany's task, even if England in her policy in Egypt overstepped the limits of discretion, to embroil herself with other Powers to please England. Moreover, regard for France and Russia forbade Germany actively to support British desires. At the same time, Bismarck reiterated his oft-repeated warnings against entering into serious negotiations with England, since it was impossible for them to be carried on in secret and, without parliamentary sanction, they afforded no security. 'It is difficult', he said, 'to embark upon and conclude reliable agreements with England otherwise than in full publicity before all Europe. But such public negotiations, at the instant of their inception, and before anything has been achieved, exercise a detrimental influence upon the majority of our other European relationships.' That Bismarck followed up this statement with the declaration that he would always cultivate the friendship of England, and readily meet her advances, does not alter the fact that the entire answer amounted to a definite refusal.

Moreover, Bismarck saw no reason to renounce the freedom of action he had hitherto retained. In order to please England he did not wish to run the risk of being opposed by Russia or to take up a definite attitude in regard to France—an attitude that could only nullify his endeavours to cultivate better relations between France and Germany. Along this path he advanced. He most certainly did not desire a war between the two Western Powers; but a state of permanent rivalry between them seemed to him serviceable for German interests. It is easily conceivable that Bismarck's attitude did not please the British Government. The obvious improvement in Franco-German relations during the ministry of Jules Ferry aroused anxiety in London; an anxiety still further increased by the renewal of the Treaty of the Three Emperors in March, 1884.

At that time the tension between England and Russia increased. Russia's advance towards Merv seemed likely to result in a bloody conflict. Rumours that she had designs on Constantinople came pouring in. The conference for the regulation of the Egyptian financial question was about to be opened in London. For all these reasons the British Government must have felt it desirable to cultivate the best relations possible with the Central Powers and more especially with Germany. The question was solely one of whether and for what price Bismarck could be induced to abandon his present policy of reserve towards England. At the very outset of the negotiations it became clear in what direction the Chancellor's desires lay.

Germany was beginning at this time to explore the still unallotted parts of the world with an eye to colonization, a pursuit in which Bismarck did not engage with great willingness. To his dying day he believed that Germany ought to be, first of all, a continental European Power; that her chief efforts ought always to be directed towards the establishment of herself as such; and that she ought always to hold herself ready to meet and repulse any danger from East or West. But there was no denying the fact that Germany could not allow the opportunity to pass of acquiring territory outside Europe. Germany could not, like other Powers, readily extend her national geographical frontiers towards either sea or land, as the need of space for her rapidly increasing population became more urgent; and, therefore, for the sake of her future she could not hold back from a movement which at that time was leading to a precipitate opening up and parcelling out of Africa. As it was, Germany came tardily to a table the best dishes on which had already been apportioned, and she had to resign herself to accept isolated and unclaimed scraps which at first sight appeared to have little nourishing value. This step, tardily and unwillingly taken, was undoubtedly of the greatest importance, as Bismarck himself realized. He knew that each extension overseas of Germany would of necessity react strongly on his policy as a whole.

Furthermore he knew that Germany could only hope to achieve a colonial policy if England permitted her to embark upon one—or at least placed no difficulties in her way. Since he judged the general situation at this time to be opportune for Germany, he did not hesitate to approach the British ministry with his demands. But he came not as one asking a favour. 'Timidity', he once said, 'cuts no ice with the want of consideration shown by British colonial policy and will never lead to enduring friendly relations with England.' Again and again he let it be known in London that a continued disregard for German colonial interests would compel him to undertake an investigation into England's actions in other directions. At the moment when he demanded the cession of Heligoland, in addition to the recognition of the German protectorate over Angra Pequena, he stated with unmistakable emphasis 'that Germany's attitude towards the opponents and rivals of England must be of greater value for British policy than the possession of Heligoland and the old rivalry between German and British commercial firms in far-distant seas'. 'England', he added, 'can make sure of the continuance of our valuable support in her political interests by making small, and for herself almost worthless, sacrifices. We shall be careful in the future, as for the past twenty-two years, to be the friends of those who are friends to us. If we should not be the friends, we should still not be the enemies of England. But it would be easy for us to be serviceable to the natural and permanent enemies of England—a service by which we should undoubtedly promote our good relations with them.' It is easy to see that, apart from the content, the form in which Bismarck stated the price for the support he was willing to give to England was bound to hurt the susceptibilities of the British ministers.

Nevertheless the general situation was such as to force them, unwillingly, and after initial opposition, to give way step by step to Bismarck in his demands. First they recognized the German claim to Angra Pequena and supported Bismarck's attitude in the Fiji Islands question. Later, under the influence of the united front presented by the Continental Powers at the conference in London about Egypt, in which England found herself faced by the opposition of the Triple Alliance and France—an opposition strengthened by the Franco-German understanding in regard to West Africa—the British ministers made still further concessions. But it was not until March, 1885, that a compromise was achieved by which, indeed, not all the difficulties were overcome, but in which Germany's right to colonization was recognized in principle. It is unquestionable that the reason for England's conciliatory policy is to be found in the precarious situation in which the British statesmen found themselves at this time. French rivalry in Egypt and West Africa, no less than the ever-growing threat from Russia in Central Asia, compelled the British Government to hold fast to the bonds that bound them to the Central Powers, although a bitter after-taste due to Bismarck's attitude remained in England that rendered still more difficult the *rapprochement* to which the events of the time were forcing the two Powers.

At that time the resignation of Ferry was a clear indication that the French colonial policy had passed its zenith. Germany was forced to reckon in an ever-increasing degree with the danger threatening from the West. Were France to make concessions to England in Egypt and the Congo, it was not impossible that a compromise with

England might be achieved to which Gladstone's Franco-phil tendencies would contribute. Such a compromise between France and England would both lessen the value of German friendship to England and obscure the prospect that England would go still further in her concessions to the colonial aspirations of Germany. Still less desirable in the interests of Germany was any prospect of success for Gladstone's attempts at a settlement of the British-Russian dispute, since thereby the basis would be laid for a very dangerous coalition of the Western Powers and Russia. Hence Bismarck avoided any step that could render Russia suspicious of the sincerity of German policy. He declared in Vienna that the future of the Straits was in the first place a matter of concern to England, and that it was not for the Central Powers to be the first to 'bell the cat and to act as the policemen of Europe'. As a consequence of this attitude on the part of Germany, which found its echo in Vienna, Gladstone and Granville felt themselves compelled to proceed with the negotiations with Russia. But since Russia revealed herself as unwilling to make concessions, the opposition to Gladstone increased. On June 5, 1885, his Government fell. His successor, Lord Salisbury, showed a desire to come to an understanding with the Central Powers. Shortly before he became Prime Minister he had said to the Austrian ambassador that a policy such as that followed by Gladstone, Granville, and Derby would never succeed. The league of England, Germany, and Austria-Hungary would be certainly a league of peace. Bismarck reciprocated Salisbury's friendly disposition with the reserve that it was not possible for him to sacrifice his good relations with Russia. Nevertheless, that the improvement in Anglo-German relations was of service to England was shown in the Egyptian question as well as in the course of the renewed negotiations with Russia.

The agreement concluded in September, 1885, between the representatives of Russia and England, turned out to be more favourable for England than had been foreseen a few months previously. But the question was whether Salisbury's cautious diplomacy would in the end lead to more momentous agreements with the Central Powers. That could only be proved when complications arising in Eastern Europe compelled the European Great Powers to take the one or the other side. The event which not only convulsed Eastern Europe, but also began most decidedly to influence the policy of all the Great Powers, was the union of Bulgaria and East Rumelia, in September, 1885. The Sultan, who, as ruler of East Rumelia, was the individual most interested, found himself at loggerheads with the two other rival Great Powers in the Balkans—Russia and Austria-Hungary. Russia had long considered Bulgaria to be her special sphere of influence; and she had been ready to promote the strengthening of this state as long as Alexander of Battenberg, Bulgaria's sovereign, remained the Tsar's vassal. Now, when Alexander attempted to assert his independence, Russia enforced his deposition. The Bulgarians, however, rebelled against Russia's candidate for the throne of Bulgaria, and Russian efforts to enforce his candidature met also with insurmountable opposition from Austria-Hungary. The old rivalry between the two Great Powers became more violently active, and despite the fact that they were united in the League of the Three Emperors, a breach opened between them.

Under these circumstances it became of the first importance to know the attitude that England and Germany would adopt in this question. England, in consideration of the general political situation which had culminated in the rivalry between Russia and herself, took the part of Russia's adversaries and became the supporter of that Greater Bulgaria whose creation she had so hotly opposed when it had been proposed by Russia at the Congress of Berlin. Her reason for this change of policy, as the British ambassador at Constantinople, Sir William White, said, was that a Bulgaria consolidated on a national basis afforded the best defence against an advance on the part of Russia. Another reason lay in the kinship between Bulgaria's deposed sovereign and the English royal family.

Nevertheless there were British statesmen like Churchill and Sir Robert Morier, then ambassador at St. Petersburg, who vented the opinion that it was not in England's interest to hinder the advance of pan-Slavism in Europe. Such an advance could only promote England's anti-Russian policy in Asia. But Salisbury, who since August, 1886, was once more directing British policy, was inspired by anti-Russian feelings. Under these circumstances the attitude adopted by Germany was bound to exercise the greatest influence upon the policy of England. How Bismarck envisaged the situation at this time is well known. The fate of Bulgaria was for him—as he said—of as little interest as that of Hecuba for the player in Shakespeare's *Hamlet*. He was resolved to maintain Austria-Hungary in her position as a Great Power, because he saw this to be an absolute necessity for Germany. But he was no less determined that Germany should be used by Austria-Hungary against Russia only in so far as it was to Germany's interests to be so used. Moreover, he had voiced the opinion that Bulgaria came within Russia's sphere of influence. Besides, he had no desire definitely to fall out with Russia to please England. At the moment, the maintenance of as friendly relations as possible with Russia appeared to be the most important consideration, since the outbreak of war between Germany and Russia would be followed by a declaration of war on Germany by France. For Paris at that time was largely under the sway of men who burned to avenge Sedan. The sound policy for Germany to pursue in her own interests was, therefore, a policy that aimed at preventing, if that were at all possible, a war between Russia and Austria-Hungary; but should this policy prove unsuccessful, then to create a situation in which Austria, without involving Germany in armed participation in the war, could hope to withstand her more powerful enemy. The sole Power which could give Austria the support necessary to afford her such a hope was England. Time and again Bismarck warned the Viennese statesmen under no circumstances to go to war with Russia unless they were previously assured of the active support of England. In September, 1886, he remarked: 'England is forever harping on the same string, that she is only a sea-power and that, therefore, in questions which concern the dry land she is of but secondary importance. If England refuses to take the lead, it would be unwise of Vienna to count upon her support in a conflict with Russia. In such an event England would leave Austria-Hungary in the lurch.' The Austro-Hungarian Government readily acted upon Bismarck's suggestion. Negotiations with reference to the Bulgarian question, which took place between the Governments of London and Vienna in 1886, had as their aim an agreement between the two states upon their attitude in conflicts which might result from the chaos existing in the Balkan Peninsula. Salisbury recognized that in order to find a *modus vivendi* it was necessary for England to return to her traditional policy in the Balkans. Malet, who was British ambassador at Berlin, voiced the same opinion, and declared that for England to allow the Russians to take Constantinople—as the new radical party desired— would be highly detrimental to British interests. The exponent of the contrary opinion was Churchill, who had, not entirely without some foundation in reason, posed the following question: 'Who will assist us against Russia in Asia, when we have secured peace in the Near East and in consequence brought upon ourselves alone the enmity of Russia?' But Churchill resigned towards the end of 1886, and Salisbury, through fear of finding England isolated, began to seek closer relations with the Triple Alliance.

Next there arose the danger that Russia would ally herself
with France, and that the two allies would make war upon
England, if Bismarck—as he often informed the British
Government—in view of the continuance of England's
passive attitude, fulfilled the demands of Russia in regard
to the Dardanelles, and by means of pressure upon Austria
compelled that Power to effect a compromise with Russia.

For a long time past Italy had been negotiating in London for an *entente*. The Austro-Hungarian ambassador at
London expressed himself in the same sense, while the
endeavours of both Austria and Italy were supported by
Bismarck. Again and again he voiced his desire that England should abandon her policy of non-intervention: otherwise she would find herself completely isolated. 'If England', he said, 'holds herself aloof from any participation
in European politics, then Germany no longer has any
reason for withholding from France and Russia the fulfilment of their desires in respect to Egypt and the East—no
matter how far-reaching those desires may prove to be.' He
expressly mentioned the possession of Constantinople as
the price for the friendship of Russia. Germany could do
no more, he said, than hold France aloof from all intervention. 'If, however, this should come about, the possibility
both for England and for Italy of a free hand would be
created; and if both these Powers, in alliance with Austria,
were strong enough to be able in all likelihood to prevent
Russia from upsetting the peace, and if, on the other side,
Germany and France would balance one another so nicely
that the sword of one keeps that of the other in its scabbard, then the balance of power and the peace of Europe
will be assured. It all depends upon England.'

Bismarck's attitude was, indeed, not the deciding factor
in making Salisbury take the step he now took; but it is
possible that the very reserve which characterized Bismarck's conduct contributed to induce Salisbury to take
the initiative. In February, 1887, an agreement was

arrived at between England and Italy which had for its object the maintenance of the *status quo* in the Mediterranean, Adriatic, Aegean, and Black Seas. England undertook to protect Italy's long coast-line from bombardment by the French fleet. Italy pledged herself to further England's interests in Egypt. A few weeks later Austria-Hungary also became a party to this agreement, of which the object was expressly stated to be the maintenance of the existing situation in the whole Mediterranean, where Austro-Hungarian interests were of paramount consideration. 'This agreement constituted a second Triple Alliance, an exact counterpart of the League of the Three Emperors, then still in operation.' England, Italy, and Austria-Hungary had in this agreement a guarantee for their separate interests; Austria-Hungary against Russia, Italy against France, and England against Russia and France. Italy could now without fear continue her Triple Alliance policy, while at the same time Germany undertook in the renewal of the Triple Alliance in February, 1887, far-reaching obligations to support Italy in the event of a Franco-Italian war. And Austria-Hungary could see the League of the Three Emperors lapse that spring without having to bestir herself to renew it. But how did Germany stand with respect to these agreements? Anxiety for Germany's position in the West in relation to France had dictated Bismarck's encouragement of these agreements and had induced him a few months later to assist at the conclusion of an Italo-Spanish agreement, and to support this in Vienna. This agreement was advantageous to England in that it denoted a strengthening of the opposition to any extension of French power in the Mediterranean. But Bismarck refused to be drawn into taking the step that would most have served England's interests—that of an avowed anti-Russian policy. For this reason he kept in the background in the Balkan problems, and did not take part in the agreements between England, Austria-

Hungary, and Italy. The same reasons caused him to refuse Italy's proposal to unite her allies with England by means of definite conditions to be laid down in a renewal of the Triple Alliance. Bismarck still believed that a war, even a victorious war, against Russia would bring no lasting benefit to Germany; that Germany's interests demanded the preservation of friendly relations between the two empires. And because he was so convinced, he resolved when the League of the Three Emperors lapsed, on one of the most daring negotiations of his life. He signed, behind Austria-Hungary's back and against the interest of England, in June, 1887, a secret treaty with Russia, in which the two Great Powers gave mutual guarantees of benevolent neutrality in the event of either of them going to war with a third power. Two exceptions were made; the guarantee of benevolent neutrality was to be disregarded by Germany if Russia undertook an aggressive war against Austria-Hungary, and by Russia if Germany made war on France. Germany was not bound to remain neutral in the event of a war between England and Russia: a clause that was all the more inimical to British interests inasmuch as Bismarck had recognized Russia's historical prerogatives in the Balkans. He pledged himself, furthermore, to give moral and diplomatic assistance to the Tsar, should he deem it necessary for the safety of his Empire to defend the entrance to the Black Sea. Neither Austria nor England had any knowledge of the existence of this Russo-German agreement, which later came to be known under the name of the Reinsurance Treaty. If it had become known in London, a break between England and Germany would very probably have followed. As it was, the refusal of Bismarck to join in measures which could only increase the danger to Germany of being involved in a war on two fronts—since he always firmly believed that France would seize the first opportunity to win back the lost provinces—produced a bad effect in London. Salisbury believed that he could bring pressure to bear on Bismarck by giving him to understand that England, at the cost of sacrifices to herself, could come to an understanding with Russia. But Bismarck, in the knowledge that Russia's support was secured to him, refused to be moved from the path in which he had resolved to tread. When the conflict between London and St. Petersburg was intensified by the election of the Prince of Coburg as Prince of Bulgaria, Bismarck declared that 'in Bulgarian questions we are in accord with Russia; in Serbian with Austria; and in Egyptian matters with England'. It was in accordance with his policy, however, to have always two irons in the fire. While he sought by all the means in his power to prevent a war with Russia, he nevertheless did not neglect the measures by which his Allies would be assured of active support in an eventual war with Russia. It was for this purpose that he lent his support to the Italian and Austrian plan of including Turkey as a fourth Power in a Mediterranean Agreement directed against Russia. This plan came to naught in consequence of Salisbury's fear of an indiscretion on the part of Turkey. At the desire of Austria-Hungary and Italy, Bismarck resolved to open negotiations afresh. This time he refrained from proposing the inclusion of Turkey, and the negotiations resulted in the drafting of a treaty containing eight articles. The signatories pledged themselves to the maintenance of the *status quo*, especially as regarded Bulgaria and the Straits, in the Near East, and announced their right to occupy suitable strategic localities for the purpose of achieving this aim. While Bismarck did his best to win the consent of the British Cabinet to this plan, he persisted in his belief that both in her own interest as well as in that of the maintenance of peace in Europe Germany could not be a party to it. His attitude aroused once more the distrust of the British ministers in the sincerity of his policy, and their fear that were England at any time involved in war with Russia she might find herself confronted with a Russo-German alliance. In order to quiet public opinion in England, Salisbury demanded from Bismarck definite pledges, a written approval of the eight articles drafted in Constantinople, and the communication in confidence of the terms of the Austro-German alliance. Bismarck replied to Salisbury in a letter dated November 22, 1887, in which many students have thought to find an offer of an alliance on the part of the Imperial Chancellor. To-day there can be no question that this letter served no other aim than to overcome Salisbury's anxiety in regard to the conclusion of the new Mediterranean Agreement. That the letter was written in so vigorous a style was due to the deterioration that had then set in in Russo-German relations; a deterioration made manifest in the articles in the Russian Press, in the publication of forged letters purporting to reveal Bismarck's duplicity in the Bulgarian question, and in expressions of sympathy with France.

'The preservation of Austria-Hungary as a Great Power', Bismarck wrote to Salisbury, 'is a necessity to Germany. Austria is as much one of the contented, peaceful, conservative nations as are the Germany and England of to-day. Austria and England have most loyally acknowledged the *status quo* of the German Empire, and have no interest in weakening it. France and Russia, on the other hand, appear to threaten us; France in that she still holds to the traditions of a hundred years ago which indicated her neighbour as her enemy; Russia in that to-day she has taken up an attitude towards Europe which threatens European peace, and which characterized the France of Louis XIV and Napoleon I.'

Then Bismarck went on to point out that for Germany there existed only one way by which she could avoid the danger of a war on two fronts, namely, through an understanding with Russia. But in order to quiet the anxiety of Salisbury he immediately added:

'But as long as we are not certain that we shall be abandoned by those Powers whose interests are identical with our own, no German Emperor can follow any other political course than that of protecting the independence of allied Powers who, content with their present circumstances, are yet ready to act without hesitation or weakness should their independence be threatened.'

In order to meet Salisbury's wishes he informed him of the content of the Austro-German Alliance of October 7, 1879, in the same form in which he had previously communicated it to Russia. Moreover, he spared himself no effort to allay Salisbury's anxiety regarding a change in Germany's foreign policy. But he persisted in his declaration that Germany would avoid a Russian war 'for so long as it is compatible with our honour and safety. We desire, however, that the friendly Powers, who have interests to safeguard in the East that are not our interests, should consider themselves strong enough to make Russia keep her sword in its scabbard, or if necessity arise, to oppose her'. Salisbury, nevertheless, immediately perceived that the Imperial Chancellor's explanations, drawn up though they were in so friendly a tone and conciliatory though they seemed to be in many respects, proved how little Bismarck was inclined at once and actively to proceed against Russia in order to defend British interests in the East. The opposing standpoints of the two statesmen were made very apparent in Salisbury's reply to Bismarck. Bismarck was the protagonist of the belief that on the outbreak of a Franco-German war Russia would take the side of France. Hence he desired that in such an eventuality England should march against Russia with Germany's allies, whilst Germany conducted the war against France. Salisbury, on the contrary, thought that Russia would utilize the favourable situation which a Franco-German war would create for her, not to enter into the war, but to 'compel the Sultan, by occupying the Balkans or Asia Minor, to accept proposals which could make Russia master of the Straits'. Russia would only abstain if she had to reckon with superior opposition. For this England and Italy would not suffice and British opinion would probably not support war for Turkey with Italy as sole partner. All would therefore depend on Austria, and unless she were sure of German support, she would not venture on war, since Italy and England could not help her in an invasion of Russia. From this it very naturally followed that Salisbury thought the best way of warding off the Russian danger would be German support to Austria. This support seemed to him to have been secured by the Austro-German Treaty of 1879 and by the agreement of Germany to the conclusion of the treaties that closely bound England with Austria and Italy. 'The grouping', he said, 'of the Powers, which is the work of the last year, will be a real buttress against Russian aggression.' Would Salisbury's opinion have been the same had he known of the existence of the Reinsurance Treaty? Were the conditions of that Treaty, by which the Tsar was assured of a benevolent neutrality, when he advanced upon the Balkans and the Straits, reconcilable with the approval of an alliance which had for its object the thwarting of such ambitions on the part of Russia? Must Bismarck not fear to discredit both himself and his policy if his conduct should through an accident become known to the Governments in London or St. Petersburg? To-day there can be no question but that this moment was the most dangerous, and at the same time the most brilliant, in the whole history of Bismarck's diplomacy. The Swede, Kjellen, has pointedly said that at this moment the right hand dared not know what the left hand did. It was a dangerous course that he was pursuing. Only a navigator of Bismarck's experience and skill could hope to bring the ship of state through all the rocks and shoals into safe harbour. As the Emperor William I once remarked, Bismarck was like a man riding on horseback and juggling with five

balls, of which he never let one fall. Success came, and
with it the apparent justification of his actions. Salisbury
agreed to the Mediterranean Treaty, which was signed on
December 12, 1887. England therewith abandoned the
passive policy she had hitherto followed, and engaged
herself in as binding a form as was possible, since the assent
of Parliament could not be asked for, to an active participation in the conflicts that might arise in the Balkans. As
is well known, the danger passed away. Bismarck was
successful in outmanœuvring the politicians in Berlin and
Vienna who were urging a war, and his warning to the war-
agitators in St. Petersburg did not fail of effect. This warning found its expression in the famous words of his speech to
the Reichstag in February, 1888, in which he said: 'If Russia
attacks the Central Powers, the whole of Germany from the
Memel to the lake of Constance will rise in a blaze, bristling
with arms, and no enemy will dare to show fight to this *furor
teutonicus*.' Russia gave way. Peace was safeguarded—to the
satisfaction most certainly of British statesmen, to whom the
prevention of a war was no less desirable than to Bismarck.

The accession to the throne of William II, following
upon the deaths in swift succession of William I and
Frederick III, led to a closer *rapprochement* between Berlin
and London. This *rapprochement* was all the more welcome
in London since the intensification of the disputes between
Russia and England, which had arisen out of Russia's
craving for a place on the Pacific Ocean and her conse-
quent construction of the Trans-Siberian Railway, as well
as the controversy with France over Indo-China, Madagascar, and West Africa, had taken on a sharper tone.
Bismarck, indeed, had no objection to better relations with
England so long as they did not interfere with German
interests. But he also desired to avoid any break in the
improved relations between Germany and Russia. Bismarck warned the young Emperor, in whose unsteady
policy, leaning now towards Russia, now towards England,

he saw a great danger for the Empire, that he could not pursue a British, but only a German policy. It did not matter if the rivalry between England and Russia continued; it mattered not at all—according to Bismarck's oft-repeated opinion—if Russia took possession of the Bosphorus, and thus was brought into conflict with the Western Powers. Bismarck's aim was, and always remained, the isolation of France. If he now succeeded in concluding with England, who had not only the rivalry of Russia but also that of France to fear in the world, an agreement directed against France, the net would be drawn close; the fear of a war of revenge on the part of France would be banished. I must confess, however, I am unable to understand how Bismarck could have hoped to win over England to the conclusion of an alliance exclusively directed against France. With great emphasis he did, indeed, seek to bring home to the British ministers the fact that a war between England and Russia would not offer a serious threat to the British world-power until the moment when France ranged herself with England's opponent. 'If it were now definitely agreed', he said, 'that by means of a German alliance England would be secure against a French attack, and Germany through an alliance with England secure against a French attack, I should consider the peace of Europe safe for the duration of such a publicly-announced alliance.'

No word is said here of the participation of Germany in a war between England and Russia, while the fact that Bismarck proposed a public alliance, sanctioned by Parliament, instead of a secret treaty between the two Governments, shows that he had no intention that Germany should take upon herself in this treaty any obligation which could give her Russian neighbour cause for complaint. The proposal was most politely refused by Salisbury on the ground that public opinion would not sanction the pursuance of so active a policy. He added that he was very grateful for the suggestion, and hoped he would live to see the time when he could accept it. 'Meanwhile we leave it on the table, without saying Yes or No, which is, unfortunately, all I can do at present.' That Bismarck had reckoned upon the probability of a refusal is shown by a remark he made at the inception of the negotiations to the effect that the refusal of his proposal would in no way influence the relations between England and Germany. Hence he was satisfied with the results of his policy. England had taken upon herself a greater responsibility in regard to Europe than she had done for many a long day past; and Bismarck could hope that he had thereby lessened the danger of a war on two fronts. Certainly there remained differences enough and to spare, but these did not prevent Anglo-German relations from remaining on a friendly footing up to the dismissal of Bismarck in March, 1890. But that is not to say that Bismarck's policy met with approval in all sections of British political opinion. I might at this point refer to a remark made by Chamberlain to the Austro-Hungarian ambassador, Count Deym, in which Chamberlain spoke in a most decided manner against a policy which might result in involving England in war with Russia without her being certain of the support of Germany.

'We do not', said Chamberlain, 'want any repetition of the Crimean war in which we pulled the chestnuts out of the fire. Naturally that would please Prince Bismarck. Our relations with Germany do not please me in the least. Prince Bismarck requires us for his colonial policy and misuses us. Germany's policy is an egotistical policy. Bismarck barters like a Jew; he insists upon being paid in advance for each service. All agreements with Germany are for the day—and not for the future. If the day came when we needed German help, we could not reckon upon receiving it. We cannot trust Bismarck. If his friendship for England is sincere, why doesn't he proffer an alliance in which we should be guaranteed German help in the event of our being involved in war?'

To Deym's rejoinder, which combated Chamberlain's opinion that England must hold herself aloof from Continental politics, Chamberlain replied: 'We do not wish to be involved in a war with Russia in which Germany will play the part of the spectator and subsequently of the arbitrator. If Germany and Austria desire to proceed against Russia, we are prepared to conclude with them both an alliance designed to meet this eventuality.' Here one sees the old game: England sees in Russia, Germany in France, the arch-enemy. A compromise was impossible, although that fact did not prevent Bismarck, shortly before his downfall, from describing England as the old and traditional ally between whom and Germany there were no contending interests.

Now let us look at the situation of England and the other Great Powers at the moment when the great statesman retired into private life. What we shall see will be something like this: Germany was then undoubtedly the centre of gravity of the Great European alliances, Austria-Hungary immediately at her side, Italy and Roumania next, England on the extreme left of the Triple Alliance; Russia in touch with Germany on the extreme right, Spain on the south-west, and Serbia on the south-east, completed the formation. 'But a closer observer could detect in this great unity two distinct groups. The one—Germany, Italy, England, Spain—directed more against France; the other—Austria-Hungary, Italy, England, Roumania—more against Russia.' This system of alliances promised England the friendship of Italy, Spain, and Germany, if her permanent differences with France should lead to a war between England and France. But in a war provoked by Russia, England could not reckon on the active support of Germany while the German Government remained faithful to Bismarck's policy. From this standpoint the dismissal of Bismarck could only be desired by England; all the more so since it was hoped that the Emperor

William II and Bismarck's successor, Count Caprivi, would steer a new course that would lead towards a *rapprochement* with England. A happy prospect appeared to have opened out, promising prosperity for both States and the continuance of the peace of the world. The circumstances that brought about the destruction of these hopes are the subject of the next lecture.

LECTURE III
(1890–1897)

WHEN the German-Russian Reinsurance Treaty, which expired in June, 1890, was not renewed, this signified a turn in German policy. Unquestionably this decision on the part of Berlin was in a large measure prompted by a desire to remove the difficulties in the way of closer relations with England, a step especially desired by Germany's allies, Austria-Hungary and Italy. Caprivi was the active exponent of this new policy in Germany. Convinced that Germany would have to face war on two fronts, he believed, as Bismarck did, in avoiding everything that might lead to a misunderstanding with England. He also desired to win England's adherence to the Triple Alliance. An agreement with England on colonial questions seemed to Caprivi the avenue of approach. In 1884, Bismarck had suggested that England should cede Heligoland to Germany, but nothing came of the project. In March, 1889, the question again arose. This time Chamberlain made advances and proposed to Herbert Bismarck—then Secretary for Foreign Affairs—the exchange of German South-West Africa for Heligoland. The Kaiser was enthusiastic, but Bismarck advised caution. 'We must wait for England's initiative at a time when England needs us', he maintained. 'Hitherto, *we* have needed *England* to preserve peace.'

Knowing that the Kaiser had set his heart on possessing Heligoland—the strategic importance of which had increased since the cutting of the Kiel canal, begun in 1887—Caprivi renewed negotiations. The British Government seemed sympathetic but demanded in return large concessions in Africa. William the Second and his Chancellor were prepared to make sacrifices; the former for reasons of personal ambition and the latter to make a permanent friend of England. As soon as the news of the signing of the treaty, concluded at the end of June, 1890, became known, a deluge of reproach against the leading statesmen in both countries broke forth. The champions of Germany's colonial policy were both furious and puzzled by the Government's action and one of them observed: 'Germany has given two kingdoms in exchange for a bath tub.' In England, Salisbury had to defend himself by declaring that Heligoland was of no strategic value. He argued that if England were at war with Germany, Heligoland would be seized before the British fleet could arrive, and he declared its value to be purely sentimental. I think that the importance of Heligoland was underestimated by both Salisbury and the representatives of the German colonial party, as was shown in the World War when the island proved a most valuable base for the German fleet. At the time when the exchange was made, however, there was no thought on either side of the North Sea of an Anglo-German war. The desire for permanent good relations was sufficient reason for Germany's giving way to English demands, and Salisbury stated: 'We have made an agreement which removes all danger of conflict and strengthens the good relations of two nations, who by their sympathies, interests, and origin will always be good friends.'

In view of the friendly feeling between the two Governments, the signing of the treaty gave rise to the hope of even closer co-operation—all the more since the differences between England and France and Russia were increasing. Simultaneously the ill-feeling against Germany increased in St. Petersburg, and it was widely rumoured in Russian circles that secret anti-Russian agreements had been made between London and Berlin. Such rumours had no foundation in fact. But it is true that when the Triple Alliance was renewed in 1891, the Central Powers endeavoured to gain England's adherence. Italy again took the chief initiative and, as before, was supported in her efforts by Austria-Hungary. Unfortunately the documents, so far published, do not permit us to trace accurately the course of these negotiations. But it is certain that Caprivi, adopting Bismarck's policy, supported the efforts of his allies who sought to renew the agreement of 1887 between Austria-Hungary, Italy, and England. Even more was planned. In a protocol appended to the third treaty of the Triple Alliance, dated May 18, 1891, it was expressly stated that an attempt must be made to bind England more closely. Germany engaged, by virtue of this treaty, to support Italy's interests in North Africa in the event of a conflict with France, and even in the case of war in *Europe* between these powers, to regard the *casus foederis* as applying. The allies now sought a similar engagement from England. The assent of England, it was stated, had already been acquired in principle to the engagements relating to the Near East, i.e. the territories of the Ottoman Empire. It was now hoped to manœuvre England into an analogous agreement with regard to the North African territories bordering on the central and western parts of the Mediterranean, and especially with regard to Morocco. The inclusion of Morocco was of the greatest importance to England because British and French interests conflicted there. The Moroccan question had already been discussed between the representatives of Germany and England. But Germany had always expressed herself with reserve. In July, 1891, the question was once more brought up in the course of a conversation between the Secretary of State for Foreign Affairs, Marschall, and Salisbury. The English statesman did not attempt to conceal the fact that Russia's designs on the Straits and France's intentions in Syria and Morocco were disquieting to him, and that he also viewed with concern the attitude of France in regard to Egypt. He did not make a definite proposal, but Marschall could not fail to see that the British Prime Minister would have welcomed a binding promise from Germany to support actively England's

interests. Marschall did not wish to commit himself to that
extent, however, and he thought that he was acting in the
Bismarckian spirit if he merely expressed his view that
Germany had no interest in Morocco. He added that in
the Near East it was England's affair to defend Constantinople against the Russians. If Germany were to interfere
there, she would be risking war on both fronts. Once
again we see how conflicting interests rendered common
action difficult in spite of the fact that both statesmen
greatly desired close relations. Nevertheless, friendly
feeling continued uninterruptedly between the two Governments; and the speeches of William II, in which he again
and again emphasized his good will towards England,
helped to make the relations between the two courts increasingly cordial. The further course of events, however,
was largely determined by the fact that the Tsar considered
the renewal of the Triple Alliance, and England's approach
towards the latter, a danger. This induced him to lend an
ear to those of his advisers who for a long time had been
working towards closer relations with France. It could
not have been easy for him, as defender of the Divine Right
of Kings, and an absolute monarch, to enter into closer
relations with republican France. But by degrees he
overcame his aversion. Perhaps Alexander the Third's
personal feelings were the same as those of William the
Second, who wrote to Alexander's son—Nicholas the
Second—in 1905, that he could not associate with men like
Loubet and Delcassé as he could with persons of his own
rank; but Alexander III acted differently from the German
Emperor. He invited the French fleet to visit Kronstadt,
where he boarded the flagship and stood up while the
band played that passionate revolutionary song, 'La
Marseillaise'. Soon afterwards, in August, 1891, agreements between the two Great Powers were concluded.
They were of a general nature, with the maintenance of
peace and the European balance of power as their object.

At the same time, no definite alliance was entered into; 'no engagement, no marriage settlement' as a modern scholar expresses it. But there is no doubt that the Tsar took a decisive step which he could not retrace. The agreement was unquestionably directed above all against Germany, and this fact came out even more pointedly in the conclusion of a Franco-Russian military convention in 1892. It is also clear that, as far as Russia was concerned, antagonism against the British Empire played a decisive part. The British statesmen viewed the future with concern. Lord Grey of Fallodon, in his Memoirs, describes the feeling which prevailed in British Government circles at that time. 'There was', he writes, 'from 1892–3 constant friction and hostility between Great Britain, France, and Russia, which might have led to a quarrel on the slightest provocation. The ground-swell of ill-will never ceased. British interests touched those of France and Russia in many parts of the world, and where interests touch, an atmosphere of ill-will is always to be feared.' Under these circumstances, an alliance between England and Germany would have been to the advantage of both nations. Nor were attempts in this direction lacking. Caprivi showed a disposition to foster friendship with England by making subsequent concessions in colonial matters. In October, 1893, an agreement respecting North Africa was arrived at by which Germany gave England a free hand in the entire Nile region, a concession the more important to England, since she was at that time preparing for the campaign in the Soudan. In return England offered to allow Germany to open up the Cameroons in the interior of Africa. In regard to other territories, also, attempts to reach agreements were made; but without success. The defeat of the Conservative Party, and their replacement by the Liberals under Gladstone's leadership, made the course of the negotiations more difficult. Gladstone was an enemy of Turkey and sought to adjust matters with Russia. Germany endeavoured to strengthen her relations with Turkey, who offered her commercial advantages. It was also known in Berlin that Gladstone and many of his colleagues sympathized with democratic France more than with conservative Germany. However, the negotiations which were conducted with the new Secretary of State for Foreign Affairs, Lord Rosebery, made it clear that the latter—though always with the caution necessitated by the feelings of the Prime Minister— was moved by a desire to win Germany for a concerted policy. When relations with France became more and more strained, owing to the differences in Egypt, Mada- gascar, and Siam, he expressed the wish to co-operate as closely as possible with Germany; a little later he even spoke of the possibility of a quadruple alliance between England and the Triple Alliance. Again the negotiations failed, because, while the interests of both countries ran parallel in many respects, in others they were very much at cross-purposes. Germany wished to avoid all conflict with France at that time, and was in nowise willing to become involved in war with Russia for the sake of England. Rose- bery, however, wanted to be sure that the Triple Alliance would stand behind him if, in the event of a Russian attack on the Straits, he were compelled to send the British fleet thither. In Berlin, however, it was feared that England, as soon as she had obliged Germany and her allies to come to England's assistance, would let the burden of a war against Russia fall upon Germany. There- fore, the German Chancellor warned Vienna and Rome, as Bismarck had frequently done, not to pledge themselves to active measures so long as England herself was not irrevocably committed. And the German statesmen also followed up the policy of Bismarck by pointing to the difficulties in the way of effectively binding England. They argued that without mutual pledges it would always remain impossible to come to an understanding on questions involving the entire strength and existence of one of the contracting powers. 'We cannot subordinate our policy to the principle of British constitutional law, nor can our allies do so', was the slogan. In vain Austria-Hungary and Italy—the former on account of Russia, the latter because of France who might desire an agreement with England—endeavoured to bring pressure to bear upon Berlin in favour of the British propositions. The German statesmen opposed all efforts to make them change their policy. There can be no doubt but that the German attitude was affected in no small degree by the British Government's attitude in the colonial questions then pending. In the Walfisch Bay affair, and especially in the issue over Samoa, Germany received no support from England. In September, 1893, Hatzfeldt was instructed to tell Rosebery that Germany would feel obliged to exercise greater reserve in her general attitude towards England, unless England took up a different attitude towards Germany's colonial interests. And in the following months the differences increased. The Congo Treaty, concluded between England and Belgium, without the consent of Germany, in May, 1894, by virtue of which England ceded Bahr-el-Ghazal in exchange for a territory which linked her South African possessions with Uganda, led to heated arguments. Germany as well as France protested and demanded the cancellation of the treaty, and England was obliged to give way. In addition to that, the attempts on Germany's part to approach France gave rise to considerable apprehension in England. The Franco-German treaty concerning the Cameroon frontier, in the spring of 1894, and the French treaty with the Congo State, in August, 1894, made possible by Germany's attitude, opened France's way from the Congo to the upper Nile. A serious clash of French and British interests in Central Africa thus became inevitable. England was also displeased because Germany was partly responsible for preventing Cecil Rhodes from

gaining control of the Pretoria–Lorenzo–Marques railroad. Furthermore, Germany crossed England's purposes
in Delagoa Bay. The rivalry of the two powers in Africa
became more and more obvious. Their mutual distrust
increased. The differences in extra-European territories
naturally affected the attitude of both powers on European
questions. Rosebery, who had succeeded Gladstone as
Prime Minister, was of the opinion that he could no longer
maintain his friendly attitude towards Germany. He
endeavoured to improve his relations with Russia, and
took a step in this direction by adopting a conciliatory
attitude in the North-West Frontier question. At the same
time he took pains to make it clear to the German Ambassador at London, Hatzfeldt, that it was to the interests of
Germany not to let the relations between the two nations
grow cold. But even this admonition produced no effect.
Hatzfeldt replied that he had always advocated close relations between the two countries, but so long as England
put obstacles in the way of Germany's colonial expansion,
and so long as she avoided every obligation to support
Germany in the event of a French or Russian attack, she
(England) must not expect permanent reciprocity from
Germany. Thus in the course of the year 1894 a serious
estrangement arose between the two countries. Germany
now tried to come into closer touch with Russia, and the
succession to the Chancellorship of Hohenlohe, who
favoured the idea of the Three Emperors Alliance, as well
as the succession to the Russian throne of Nicholas the
Second (more favourable to an understanding with
Germany than his father), increased the possibilities of this
move proving fruitful of results.

Events in the Far East, which vigorously reacted
upon Europe, and which were destined to influence the
development of the international policy of the European
Great Powers, offered an opportunity. In 1894, war broke
out between China and Japan, from which the latter

emerged the victor. The Japanese peace conditions were extremely exacting. China applied to the European Great Powers for mediation. At the beginning of the war England had attempted to mediate, because for economic, commercial, and political reasons, as well as from fear of an international conflict, she did not wish the Chinese Empire to be partitioned. Her efforts, however, met with no success because Russia hesitated and Germany refused to co-operate. After the conclusion of the Peace of Shimonoseki, when Russia attempted to carry England's earlier suggestion into effect, Great Britain drew back. The three Great Powers, Germany, France, and Russia, compelled Japan to restore to China the victor's most valuable conquest, the Liau-Tung peninsula, in return for an indemnity. It is important to note in connexion with this intervention on the part of the so-called Far East Triple Alliance that England did not participate. During the course of the war she had decided to draw towards the Japanese, believing that Japan was the one Power capable of holding England's rival in the East, Russia, in check. This was certainly far-sighted statesmanship. The German Government, and above all the Kaiser, took Russia's side, arguing: 'Russia will do justice to our wishes if openly supported by us.' The German representative, in contrast to the French and Russian Ambassadors at Tokio, showed a great lack of tact in the tone adopted towards the Japanese. Without question this conduct greatly influenced the attitude of the Japanese at the outbreak of the World War. It is a characteristic example of the inability of the German mind to comprehend the psychology of other people. Berlin also underestimated the bad impression produced in England by Germany's attitude in Eastern Asia. The distrust of her policy increased and was strengthened when questions concerning the Near East made it clear that the Berlin Government was unwilling to show any consideration for the interests of the Island Kingdom.

Salisbury, who had become Prime Minister and taken charge of the Foreign Office, recognized at that time the danger contained in England's isolation. The common advance of Germany, France, and Russia in the Far East; the closer relations between France and Germany, reflected by the presence of the French at the opening of the Emperor William Canal in June, 1895; as well as the Franco-German agreement in Africa, increased Salisbury's concern respecting the possibility of a continental alliance directed against England. He considered it his principal task to avoid this; the question was simply by what means the goal was to be reached. It appeared as if Salisbury thought for a time of entering into a permanent partnership with the Triple Alliance and with Germany in particular. He thought he saw a means thereto in an agreement concerning the partition of Turkey, for he assumed that the latter could not be sustained as a European Power in the long run. Salisbury had never been personally very much in favour of maintaining Turkey intact, and at this time, when the Christians had again rebelled against the Turks in Macedonia, and the Armenian question had become more acute, he doubted whether the present situation in the Near East could be long maintained. In Germany, however, there was more than one objection to this suggestion—for it was no more than a suggestion and certainly not a concrete plan. The statesmen of Germany feared the egoistic designs of the British ministers and thought that they sought to incite conflicts between the Continental Powers from which they might profit. The German Foreign Office advised Emperor William to be reserved upon this subject. He complied. Personal sensibilities, which came to light during the course of a conversation between the Emperor and Lord Salisbury at Cowes, were in part also responsible for the negative result of the negotiations. At the same time Hatzfeldt failed to refute the so-

called 'chestnut theory' of Holstein, England's strongest
antagonist.

'A war between the Continental Powers is not desired by
Salisbury,' he wrote, 'and England cannot play her former
role in this instance because, should Italy and Austria be
defeated, England would be hopelessly in the hands of Russia
and France and forced to accept all or any conditions imposed
by them. Any peace treaty made between the contending
Powers would, under such circumstances, be to the detriment
of England because she had not supported any of them. All
this is well known to Salisbury.'

But Holstein clung to his theory, and the uncompromising attitude of Germany induced Salisbury to enter into
negotiations with the Dual Entente. Constantinople *avec tout
ce qui s'en suit* for Russia, Morocco for France, was the plan.
But very soon afterwards Salisbury decided to return to his
old principle of Splendid Isolation; and when the Sultan, in
October, 1895, showed himself ready to carry out the reforms demanded in Armenia, Salisbury abandoned his plan
of partition. It may be presumed that this plan had been
built upon the assumption of a permanent union with the
Triple Alliance and above all with Germany, who was to
guard England's interests against France and especially
against Russia, whenever necessary. To this the German
statesmen did not wish to pledge themselves. 'In the face of
this sort of British policy', wrote Holstein, 'we should less
than ever consider burning our bridges leading to Russia.'
Time and again distrust of British sincerity made an agreement impossible. This showed itself in November, 1895,
when the Empress Frederick made a new attempt to win
over her son to the idea of a conference in Berlin, in which
common steps against the Sultan and a plan of partition
were to be once more discussed. William calmly listened to
the proposals of his mother, which were evidently not the
offspring of her mind, but were strangely akin to the plans
broached by Salisbury only a few months before. The

Kaiser consulted his Chancellor, who was against the conference and against any assent to England's plans. Thereupon the Emperor declined, emphasizing that 'the congress of Berlin was a great mistake; I shall never agree to another'. Upon the proposal of England for a conference of Ambassadors in Constantinople in order to formulate a concerted policy in regard to the Sultan, who had not kept his recent promise to introduce thorough reforms, he remarked: 'The insistence upon energetic steps is entirely justified because the role which we Europeans are playing towards the Moslems is more than pitiful. But that England should expect others to take steps instead of doing so herself is extremely strange, when one remembers that the entire swindle was originated by Great Britain.' Only if England herself should take the initiative would it be proper to agree to her proposals. 'The British, however, desire that we should fight for the plums which they shake off the Turkish trees.'

It is quite clear that Germany's attitude excited displeasure in London, and this was further increased by the Emperor's friendly attitude towards the Boers. The Germans, on their side, complained of the impediments which the British put in the path of their modest colonial ambitions. In the course of a conversation with the British Ambassador, Sir Edward Malet, on the occasion of his retirement from Berlin, and in a subsequent talk with the British Military Attaché, Colonel Swain, the temperamental Monarch gave vent to his indignation at the British Government's attitude. Upon Malet's remarking that England possessed the means of satisfying and appeasing many of her enemies, the Emperor replied: 'Yes, if she is willing to sacrifice the Dardanelles, Gibraltar, Malta, and Cyprus. But that is rather a high price to pay; it would be better to allow Germany some small colonial advantages.' And to Swain he remarked: 'For the sake of a few square miles of niggers and palm trees, England has actually threatened her only real friend, a grandson of Her Majesty the Queen, with war.' The Emperor intimated strongly that he would make common cause with France and Russia, in the event of Salisbury pursuing his policy, and demanded that the problems should be frankly discussed. England was either to conclude a 'sealed contract' with the Triple Alliance or else openly come out against it. When, at the beginning of December, the Italians suffered a defeat in Abyssinia and looked to England for help, William once more asked Swain if Great Britain would not join the Triple Alliance, stating that otherwise she might find herself opposed by a solid block of Continental Powers. These were threats which, without attaining their purpose, merely increased the British politicians' distrust and apprehension of a German-Russian understanding. Under these circumstances, Salisbury *would* not and *could* not burn the bridges connecting England with Russia; and therefore he adopted a reserved attitude towards the endeavours of Vienna and Rome to renew the Mediterranean agreement, which was directed against Russia and France. He did not wish to forfeit the possibility either of playing the Triple Alliance off against Russia, or of coming to terms with Russia at the expense of Turkey, in order to avoid conflict with the former in the Far East. Behind the irritation then existing in Germany and England, however, there was still another reason: the conviction in Germany that England, always bent on building up her own colonial Empire, begrudged Germany any expansion of her colonial possessions, a conviction which became increasingly deeply rooted in Germany. This expansion, however, was considered a vital necessity on account of the rapid increase in population and the need for adopting measures for the future. Even Bismarck had not been unsympathetic to these ideas during the last years of his administration, although his point of view in the matter was that Germany should obtain these advantages on colonial questions merely by the position which she took in European affairs as a great Continental Power. As a matter of fact, he succeeded by skilful exploitation of the British-Russian and British-French rivalries in wresting many a concession from the British statesmen. The Emperor William, however, was of the opinion that another road should be followed. Since his accession, his attention had been more and more engrossed in maritime affairs and the building of a fleet. After Caprivi's retirement, the Kaiser's active participation in maritime affairs increased. In 1896, during the celebration attending the twenty-fifth anniversary of the foundation of the German Empire, he said: 'It is our privilege to enjoy in a thankful spirit the advantages which my grandfather William acquired when he founded the German Empire. Our first duty must be to preserve that which he fought to gain. The German Empire has grown to be a World Empire. Wherever we may go, in all parts of the world, thousands of our countrymen have made their homes. German merchandise, German newspapers, German industry are crossing the seas. The value of German goods which are now on the high seas amounts to thousands of millions.' Shortly afterwards he said: 'Our future is on the seas.' And he was convinced that Germany needed a big fleet in order to maintain permanently her commercial and political interests, a view which was shared by many influential circles in the Empire. This big fleet, however, was not yet at the Emperor's disposal. Good relations with the leading sea power alone offered any prospect of success for Germany's colonial policy; but then the *tempo* would have to be retarded. But the leading German politicians were of the opinion that they could reach their goal by taking a different road.

The German Emperor had repeatedly threatened to conclude a Continental alliance against England. His councillors, above all Holstein, went to work to put this plan into effect. The occasion appeared to present itself in December, 1895, when Jameson crossed the frontiers of the Transvaal. Germany protested in strong language, and began negotiations in St. Petersburg and Paris to bring about united action against England. The defeat of Jameson, and Salisbury's declaration that the British Government was not connected with Jameson's undertaking, nipped the conflict in the bud. Great was the surprise and indignation in England, therefore, when a telegram of the Emperor to Kruger became known, in which he congratulated the Boer Republic's President on conquering the disturber of the peace and on defending the independence of his own country unaided and without appealing to friendly powers. This action on the part of the Emperor showed not only a lack of tact; it was also unwise. Threats are only useful when they can be followed up by deeds. Germany's efforts to establish a Continental front against England were doomed to failure from the start. In Paris the German suggestion was not only disapproved altogether, but word of it was immediately sent to London with the intimation that France knew but *one* enemy, Germany. As for Russia, she too showed little inclination to support the German project. The entire enterprise went by the board. The German Government saw itself compelled to recommend moderation to the Boers without being able to prevent England's distrust of their sincerity from increasing. If, as is said, the German statesmen were not actuated by a desire to protect their commercial interests in South Africa, nor by sympathy for the Boers in their fight for liberty, but merely by a wish to let England know that Germany was not prepared to allow any further extension of the British Empire without equivalent compensation, and that it was to England's own interests to be on good terms with the Triple Alliance— then they made a huge mistake. Salisbury declined to renew the Mediterranean agreement, so much desired by Austria-Hungary and Italy and advocated by Germany.

The Austro-Hungarian statesmen were consequently in a bad humour, because they wanted to continue to regard England as partner in a possible war against Russia, and at the same time regarded compromise with Russia—recommended by Germany—as impossible. Heated arguments took place between the two Governments, in the course of which Berlin stated—though the German statesmen hardly meant what they said—that Germany had no objection to Austria-Hungary endeavouring to conclude an alliance with England at the expense of abandoning the Triple Alliance. In Berlin it was very well known that Austria-Hungary would not dare to take this step.

Still more than the statesmen of Austria-Hungary, those of Italy lamented the estrangement between Germany and England. They partially ascribed the heavy defeat which they suffered in March, 1896, at Adowa to the attitude of the Germans, and they urgently demanded German support in their renewed attempt to obtain England's help in these times of distress. Accordingly, the Kaiser intervened in London to point out the dangers which, in his opinion, threatened England. 'First', he said, 'France is supporting Menelik; secondly, Russia intends to occupy Massowa after the expulsion of the Italians, and will block the sea road from Suez to India; thirdly, France will seize the Canary Islands and thus command the sea route round the Cape of Good Hope to India.' With these chimeras he hoped to obtain the British Government's support for Italy and her adhesion to the Triple Alliance. Salisbury, however, in view of Germany's action very politely declined the Teutonic invitation, declaring that he could not give any promise by which England would bind herself in any way to be involved in war. It was in consequence of this attitude on the part of England, as expressed by Salisbury, that the Italian Government told Vienna and Berlin that although they recognized the obligations towards the Triple Alliance agreements—the renewal of these agreements was pending at that time—they could never participate in a war in which England would fight on the side of the enemy. England profited by the occasion to inaugurate her long-planned campaign for the conquest of the Sudan: the difficulties put in her way by France and Germany did not deter her from this purpose. The tension between London and Berlin increased; distrust arose. It is significant that William the Second, in October, 1896, expressed apprehension lest England might take Germany's colonies from her. Hatzfeldt, who knew the British better, endeavoured to alleviate the Kaiser's fears by saying: 'Salisbury knows very well that if such a surprise attack took place, we should march into the Russian camp with drums and trumpets and should strengthen and encourage every hostile feeling of the Russians or the French, respectively, against England.' This statement did not fail of effect in Berlin. Nevertheless, the view of William and Hohenlohe that Germany must continue in her policy of a free hand, and must avoid all and any conflict with Russia, was strengthened. In this sense Hohenlohe and the Kaiser were active, when a new war threatened in the Balkans, due to the hopelessness of peace in Turkey. The unrest in Armenia persisted; Crete, backed by Greek support, was in revolt against the Sultan's rule; and Macedonia was the stage of continual unrest. A clash of the Great Powers seemed likely. German statesmen were of Bismarck's opinion that the Russians might be permitted to come to the Mediterranean. This would have been most inconvenient to France, on account of her Syrian interests, and would, perhaps, have loosened the ties of the Dual Alliance. In any event, however, England would be forced to take action. Only if England were seriously engaged, or offered binding pledges, would the Triple Alliance in the opinion of Berlin bestir itself. But Austria-Hungary refused to be a party to the project of delivering Constantinople to Russia. German attempts at mediation failed of success. England, of course, also did not want to see the Dardanelles in the possession of Russia; but she adopted a policy which deviated from that of the other Powers, by siding with Crete and the Greeks, just as before she had sided with the Armenians against the Turks; and she refused Germany's proposal to blockade all Greek ports so as to make support of the Cretan rebellion impossible. She kept to her policy that it was necessary to support the Christian States of the Balkans in their endeavours to free themselves from the yoke of the Mohammedans. Salisbury could not prevent the statesmen of the other Great Powers from being of a different opinion. Germany and Austria-Hungary definitely took the side of Turkey. Russia, whose Tsar in October, 1896, had told the Kaiser—even if somewhat exaggeratedly: 'I am not at all interested in Constantinople. My entire interest and my eyes are directed upon China'—proved her lack of interest in the Balkans by the conclusion, in April, 1897, of an agreement with Austria-Hungary which had for its purpose the maintenance of the *status quo* in Turkey as well as the recognition —so long refused—of Ferdinand of Coburg as Prince of Bulgaria. France and Italy more or less unwillingly backed up their respective allies. Thus England was completely isolated in the Near Eastern question and had finally to give way, under protest, to the other Powers. The Greeks saw themselves forced, after suffering defeat at the hands of the Turks, to accept the conditions of peace imposed by the victor, and, as matters stood towards the end of 1897, it actually appeared as if the Triple Alliance had coalesced with the Dual Alliance into one solid block. The Emperor William, whose imagination could not free itself from the idea of a Continental alliance, eagerly adopted the plan. Misleading information from Paris to the effect that the idea of *revenge* had subsided, as well as the very conciliatory attitude of Nicholas the Second on the occasion of a meeting with the German Emperor in the autumn of 1897, strengthened the latter in his hopes. The leading statesmen, however, did not share the views of their War-Lord. Marschall, who in June, 1897, resigned his office, was of the opinion that a Continental League could not be taken seriously by the practical politician. In his opinion, all that might come of a Continental alliance was the prevention of England's endeavours to stir up the Continent. And his successor as Secretary for Foreign Affairs, Bernhard von Bülow, was still more decided in expressing his views. The question is often asked why Germany did not seize this opportunity to conclude a Continental alliance against England, and thereby enable herself to carry through her colonial plans against the will of the Island Kingdom; secondly, why, when in the Dongola Incident the Egyptian question was brought up, Germany sided with England against Russia and France; and thirdly, why, at the time when England was preparing for her final campaign against the South African Republic,. Germany maintained an attitude friendly to England. These are all very natural questions inasmuch as England was then engaged in serious controversies with Russia in Asia, and with France in Africa, controversies which threatened her rule in India and in Egypt. The rapid advance of the Russians in China, and their economic hold on Manchuria, achieved by the extension of the Trans-Siberian railroad, created much anxiety in England, which was increased when it became known that Port Arthur, one of the most important strategic points for the domination of the Yellow Sea, had been ceded to Russia. That England later received Wei-hai-wei and an extension of her territory near Hong-Kong in compensation was not sufficient to alleviate her fears for her East Asian trade, all the more since Germany, on account of the lease of Kiao-chow and the concessions given her in the neighbouring territory regarding railroads and mines, now came forward

as a new competitor. Moreover, England's African possessions were still more endangered by the fact that in 1898,
after the conquest of the Sudan, England and France came
into direct conflict in Africa. The French, as a climax to
their brilliant African policy, had made a great advance
from West to East in order to intercept the Cape to Cairo
line, planned by the British, and they had endeavoured to
link up their own (French) colonies in Central and West
Africa. A decided stand in support of France and Russia
on Germany's part would, so the advocates of a Continental league against England maintained, place England
in such a different position that she would either have to
yield or suffer defeat. But Bülow, who, although only
Secretary of State, was already the real formulator of
Germany's foreign policy, was not of this opinion. He dis-
trusted France, believing it to be impossible permanently
to bridge over the German-French disagreements, and he
did not wish to be taken in tow by Russia. He also feared
lest Germany might be left in the lurch at the first opportunity by both these allied Great Powers. He was convinced that the diverging interests of the Danubian
Monarchy and Russia in the Balkans had not been bridged
over by the Treaty of April, 1897, but that the issue had
only been postponed; and that a permanent adjustment
was debatable. Such a settlement could probably only
have been achieved by the division of the Balkans into two
spheres of interest, a plan urged time and again by
Bismarck. But Vienna was not ready for this step. When
the German Ambassador at Vienna mentioned the idea of
a Continental League, the Minister for Foreign Affairs,
Goluchowsky, replied: 'I would never consent to it, for
Austria's *one* foe is Russia.' To this was added the attitude
of the St. Petersburg Government in the course of the
negotiations relating to Germany's obtaining a foothold in
Eastern Asia—an attitude which made it evident that
Russia agreed only under pressure of circumstances to the

demands of her Western neighbour. This was another obvious reason why Germany could not place too much reliance on Russia's good will. Hence, Bülow, for the time being, decided to maintain the policy of the free hand. He intended, if possible, to maintain friendly relations with all the Great Powers, and to leave it to the future whether the course was to be directed towards the East or towards the West. An opportunity for this decision presented itself shortly—an opportunity which could not have been better. The fate of Germany, in fact the peace of the world, depended on whether the statesmen in Berlin were capable of grasping the situation. The reasons why nothing came of the opportunity on this occasion will be made clear in the next lecture.

LECTURE IV
(1898–1902)

THE dangerous position, briefly outlined in the previous lecture, in which England found herself at the beginning of 1898, led British statesmen to seek an agreement with one or the other of England's rivals. First they approached Russia. In January, 1898, before the decision regarding Port Arthur and the British claims in East Asia had been reached, they proposed to the Russian Government to come to an understanding with reference to the British and Russian interests in the Far and in the Near East. Not a territorial division was planned, but merely a division of political influence. The Tsar, however, and his ministers did not receive the proposal in a way which inspired confidence or encouraged the British to proceed with their plan. It was, therefore, only natural that England now considered approaching Germany; all the more as at the time her conflict with France in Africa became more acute. England was completing the conquest of the Sudan. France also had her eyes on that part of Africa; while in South Africa, England's quarrel with the Transvaal Republic was approaching a crisis. The question whether the first step was taken by Germany or England cannot be decided with certainty by means of the hitherto published documents. Nor is it of any importance. But it is certain that both sides were desirous of achieving some sort of understanding. In January, 1898, Emperor William expressed to the British military attaché his desire to conclude a treaty with England. He had been striving for eight years, but without success, to bring about an alliance, he remarked with much exaggeration; and Salisbury, in a conversation with Hatzfeldt, late in 1897, stressed the fact that England's navy, however powerful, would not suffice, without a corresponding army, to bring about a decision in a Continental war. He had begun, he said, to see that England might by unforeseen events be forced to give up her policy of 'Splendid Isolation'. His cautious and hesitating manner, however, as well as his clinging to the dogma that alliances should not be concluded before they became indispensable, was responsible for his desire to postpone a decision as to whether and with whom he should enter into a permanent alliance entailing in many respects binding responsibility.

The colonial minister, Chamberlain, was of a different opinion. The British documents, as we know, do not mention Chamberlain's proposals. And since his biography has not yet appeared, we depend, so far as Chamberlain's plans of 1898 are concerned, entirely upon the German published documents and those published in Eckardstein's Memoirs. It is certain that Chamberlain was not alone in his idea of an alliance with Germany. And it is also practically certain, from what we know of Chamberlain's political ideas up to the year 1898, that he was sincere in his overtures, although he was no friend of Germany. Chamberlain was a business man. He was of the opinion that England's situation necessitated the abandonment of the policy of 'Splendid Isolation', and he believed that an Anglo-German alliance was more in the interest of the British Empire and obtainable under less exacting conditions than an alliance with France and Russia. At the very first conference he laid his cards on the table. He did not deny that there were numerous points of friction, especially where colonial questions were concerned, but he stressed the view that no vital diverging interests existed. In order to quiet Germany's fears that *later* British Cabinets might not keep the agreement, he proposed an open alliance sanctioned by Parliament. Later, he did not fail confidentially to imply that this would not prevent the inclusion of one or more secret articles in the treaty. At the same time, he made no secret of the fact that, in the event of the attempt failing, England would be obliged to negotiate with the Dual Alliance for some sort of an agreement. That the alliance, as planned by Chamberlain, was directed above all against Russia was evident; this was also intimated by him. Such an open alliance, however, was not to the liking of the German statesmen. Bülow was strongly of the opinion that it would involve Germany in a war on two fronts in which the British fleet would be able to give Germany but scant support. An even greater danger lay in the possibility of Parliament declining to sanction such an alliance. In that case it was to be feared that Germany's enemies, certain that England would not come to Germany's assistance, might more readily decide to make war on her. Moreover, many influential men in Germany, above all Holstein, had once more grown distrustful of England. They thought that she wanted to stir up a Continental war in order to profit by it. This opinion was undoubtedly erroneous. At this time England had to cope with the Russian expansion in China and with the ambitions of France in Africa. These two Powers, and *not* Germany, were actually her rivals. In her own interest England would have been obliged to side with the Triple Alliance in case of a Continental war. But the Germans naturally wanted to avoid this war; and they did not wish to break with Russia, simply because Russia's interests, diverted from Europe, clashed with those of England in Eastern Asia. This was the controlling reason for Germany's attitude of reserve, an attitude strengthened by the conviction that, as Bülow put it, war between England and Russia would sometime come with 'elementary necessity'. Therefore, Berlin thought it best to wait until England more urgently needed Germany's support and would thus be willing to pay a higher price for it. To put England off until the opportune moment, and to humour her by admitting in principle the desirability of an understanding, was considered in Berlin to be the only correct policy. 'With England friendly to us', averred William the Second, 'we retain in our hand one more trump card against Russia, and, in addition, we have every chance of obtaining colonial and commercial advantages from the Island Kingdom.' Accordingly Hatzfeldt was instructed to tell Chamberlain that a formal alliance at the moment was inopportune; but that Germany would remain neutral in return for special concessions from England, and that this would suffice to keep France neutral in the event of war between Russia and England. Chamberlain was not satisfied with this. He considered a *defensive* alliance with Germany necessary to make France and Russia change their attitude; but his opinion fell on deaf ears in Berlin. The negotiations lagged all the more because Salisbury refrained from doing anything to help them along. He did not seem to be much worried about the Russian danger in China, and would not let himself be induced to pay the high price which the conclusion of a defensive alliance with Germany would cost. He told Hatzfeldt at the time: 'You demand too much for your friendship'; and afterwards he remarked: 'alliance agreements should only be concluded when mutual interests appear seriously threatened.' He still believed that he was in a position to wait and keep his hands free. Thus it appears that Salisbury and the majority of his colleagues, like the German statesmen, did not wish to assume binding obligations tending to impede their freedom of action. However, neither side wished to break off abruptly but wished to leave the road open for future negotiations.

This did not prevent England from attempting to straighten out her difficulties with France in Africa. She succeeded, as a matter of fact, in clearing up the delicate problem of the Niger territory, although the settlement of the most difficult problem—the future of the upper Nile valley (which meant the fate of Egypt)—remained unsolved. Emperor William now decided upon a step which can only be explained by his peculiar mentality. He communicated with the Tsar—without asking the advice of his ministers—and with an exaggeration which mocked the truth told of repeated offers on the part of England for an alliance under ever increasingly favourable concessions 'which open up to my country a wide and large future . . .' 'What can and will *you* offer me if I refuse England's overtures?' was his question to Nicholas. According to Emperor William's own notes, the sudden decision to take this step, which could be justified from the point of view of neither morality nor intelligence, was born of the conviction that England had made the offer of an alliance only from fear of the consequences of the Fleet Bill which he, William, by the exertion of his entire authority had succeeded in putting through in 1897. The Kaiser thought that England wished either to force Germany to enter an alliance which would make the development of German world policy dependent on Britain's good will; or else to destroy her world trade before Germany was sufficiently strong to resist, just as centuries before she had annihilated that of Holland. It is hardly necessary to say that this was mere fantasy on the part of the Emperor, for, as we well know, the first German Fleet Bill hardly stirred British public opinion. Again, it is true that the extremely rapid expansion of German foreign trade, while raising some fears among the representatives of certain British industries, nevertheless did not have any controlling effect upon the decisions of the British Government. The often cited quotation of an English Review: *Germaniam esse delendam* found stronger repercussion in Germany than it did in England. In the meantime Emperor William met with a decided refusal in St. Petersburg. The answer of Nicholas the Second—most assuredly not his own composition— was a masterpiece of diplomatic artifice. The Kaiser was strengthened in his disinclination to conclude an alliance with England, and in his distrust of British diplomatic honesty, by a communication of the Tsar to the effect that

England, in January, 1898, had made equally tempting proposals to Russia which he (Nicholas) had at once refused. As for a reply to William's question as to what Russia would concede to Germany for refusing England's offers, there was none. Nicholas ignored that part of the communication. His attitude should have warned the Emperor, and the German politicians, to exert all their diplomatic ability towards winning England's friendship, even if it came to making sacrifices. However, they stuck to their opinion that time was working in favour of Germany and that, therefore, they would do best to cling to the policy of a free hand. 'First of all wind up colonial matters; as for the rest—wait:' was the opinion of William.

England was ready to meet Germany half-way in colonial matters. Towards the end of August, 1898, a Treaty was concluded which offered the German Empire a prospect of considerably increased possessions in Africa, namely in parts of Angola and Mozambique, if Portugal—at that time in financial difficulties—should be forced to sell her colonies. In return England obtained Germany's approval of the cession of Delagoa Bay—the key to the Transvaal. By mutually pledging themselves to oppose the intervention of any other power in Angola, Mozambique, and Timor, the treaty with Germany assumed the character and importance of an *alliance* covering this special question, directed above all against France. This might have formed the basis of a general agreement, as was the case later in the Anglo-French negotiations concerning Morocco, and the Anglo-Russian negotiations relating to Persia. As far as England was concerned, that was probably the intention. The German statesmen, however, did not wish to go further. They were afraid that a general alliance with England would embroil them with Russia in the Far East. This, in their opinion, would only serve British interests, while those of Germany were best safeguarded when Russia was kept busy in Eastern Asia; thus the danger of the Austro-Russian flame of conflict being rekindled in the Balkans would be avoided. That England would carry out Chamberlain's threats, and unite with France and Russia, was not believed in Berlin, all the more as the Anglo-Russian differences in Asia and the Anglo-French conflict in Africa appeared to be approaching a crisis. Kitchener, in September, 1898, defeated the Mahdi at Omdurman and then advanced against Marchand, who in the meantime, had arrived in the upper Nile valley and hoisted the French flag at Fashoda. A clash appeared imminent, but at the last moment the French gave way. Bülow remarked at the time: 'The humiliation of France would have been unthinkable if England had not felt perfectly sure of Germany's good will.' France had to retreat, and in March, 1899, concluded a treaty satisfactory to England. Another agreement favourable to England's interests was arrived at respecting Madagascar. At the same time the danger of an Anglo-Russian war was overcome.

Once more, it is true, the Russians brought forward the idea of a Russo-German alliance in the spring of 1899, by virtue of which Russia was to receive concessions regarding the Straits, while Germany was to have a free hand in Asia Minor, where she had been actively extending her sphere of interest for some time past. The concessions which the Anatolian Company had obtained in the course of 1889, to enable it to continue the construction of the railroad to Baghdad, proved that far-reaching and very real plans were behind the words uttered by William in Damascus in which he protested his friendship for the Sultan and the three hundred million Mohammedans. The proceedings of the Germans were everywhere regarded as constituting a very decided step towards establishing a strong industrial and economic position in Asia Minor. Russia made difficulties, but showed inclination to come to an agreement with Germany in return for corresponding concessions in the Balkans. Germany, however, declined, after long hesitation, because she did not wish to break off relations with Austria-Hungary—a break that threatened to come about if she took this step. Germany also feared to irritate England, who, as Bülow correctly observed, had hitherto not abruptly opposed the German colonial ambitions, because she hoped for Germany's neutrality in the event of an Anglo-Russian war. Under one condition *only* would the Germans have been ready for a complete change of front, namely, a guarantee of their possession of Alsace-Lorraine. This the Russian statesmen would not grant, for had they done so, they would have run the risk of having their ally, France, outraged by their deceit, unite with England, and, together with that Power and Japan, thwart Russia's plans in East Asia.

The Russian statesmen, in accordance with their own best interests, couched their refusal in the most friendly language, and declared in Berlin that France was not yet ready for a concession of that sort. At the same time, however, in August, 1899, the Russians and French prolonged and extended their military convention of 1892. And now it was not only the maintenance of world peace, but more especially the preservation of the European balance of power which was declared the purpose of the alliance. This agreement was especially directed against any possible desire on the part of Germany to increase her possessions in the event of a division of Turkey, or possibly of the Austro-Hungarian Monarchy. The failure of the attempt to come to an understanding with Germany was very likely responsible for an improvement in Anglo-Russian relations. The agreement of the two Powers with reference to China, in April, 1899, did not, it is true, bring about a definite solution of the delicate questions at issue; but it eliminated the acute danger of war. In Russia the peace party had gained the day. The first Peace Conference at the Hague, convened on the initiative of Nicholas the Second, clearly proved this.

The triumph of England over France in Africa, and the very evident inclination of Delcassé, despite the ill-humour of the French nation owing to these British successes, to smooth the way for an understanding with England, no less than the change of policy in Russia, were diplomatic successes bound to have their repercussion upon the attitude of the British Government towards Germany. There was now little inclination on the part of England to humour the colonial desires of William. The Samoan question in particular brought about conflicts which found their expression in severe attacks by the Emperor upon Salisbury, and sharp words in reply on the part of Queen Victoria. The conclusion of the Windsor Treaty with Portugal in 1899, which was not entirely compatible with the Anglo-German agreement, pointed to a parting of the ways. Even Chamberlain, the champion of an Anglo-German Entente, gave vent in April, 1899, to his displeasure at German policy when, on the occasion of the negotiations regarding Samoa, he declared: 'A year ago we offered you everything, and you declined our advances; now it is too late.' The friction increased. The Prince of Wales, during a conversation with the Austro-Hungarian Ambassador, severely criticized the conduct of William. There could never be a German-English alliance, he remarked, because the Kaiser wanted it at too high a price. Even more strongly Bertie, the Under-Secretary of State, expressed himself to Mensdorff a few months later: The Germans were like the Jews; they always wanted to get something by obstinately dickering for every petty advantage and, with it all, they were always unfriendly towards England; the Press and public opinion in Germany were decidedly anti-British; the Kaiser only friendly when he wanted something; German friendship showed itself negatively: 'If you do *that for us*, we promise not to do anything *against* you.'

There was also talk of German propaganda against

England in Russia and France, and as a matter of fact, it is true that about this time the idea of a Continental league against England was once more considered in Berlin. William the Second was again inclined to give credence to erroneous information which came to him from Paris, and to hope for an agreement with France, the basis of which was to be France's renunciation of the reconquest of Alsace-Lorraine. He was to find out very soon that the reality did not correspond with his dreams. How strongly anti-German was the character of the French Government, especially under Delcassé, how far from the truth the belief that France had forgotten the idea of *revanche* for 1871, was never fully grasped by the Kaiser.

It was understandable that Berlin gradually came to wish to be on more cordial terms with England, since the French alliance did not seem to materialize. England, too, in view of the difficult situation in which she had found herself since October, 1899, owing to the outbreak of the Boer war and her early defeats, was *still* ready to meet Germany half way. With this in view a new special treaty, favourable to Germany, the Samoa Treaty, was concluded between London and Berlin in November, 1899. The better understanding between the two Governments was reflected also in the fact that Bülow, with entire disregard for the strong pro-Boer feeling in Germany, clung to the strictest neutrality, and that the Emperor, although his indignation at the attitude of Salisbury had not entirely died away, refused a proposal, proffered by the French in October, 1899, to take common precautionary measures against the colonial appetite of England. Thus the road was free for the further attempts to bring about closer relations which were made during the sojourn of the Kaiser and Bülow in England in the last week of November, 1899. Chamberlain once more, with entire frankness, developed a plan along broad lines which contemplated the co-operation of England, the United States, and

Germany for the sake of safeguarding the mutual interests of these powers. Again the proposed alliance was directed above all against Russia, with a view to protecting China, Persia, and Turkey against the Russian desire for expansion. To this, however, neither the Kaiser nor Bülow was ready to assent, although Chamberlain's views regarding Turkey, his promise not to interfere with Germany's undertakings in Asia Minor, and his proposal regarding the participation of British capital in the Anatolian Railroad venture and the future acquisitions in Morocco—'Tangier for England, the Atlantic Coast Line for Germany'—were pleasing to both. Thus once more the efforts of the British statesmen were wrecked by the determination of Bülow and the Emperor to cling to their principle of a free hand, and by their disinclination to enter into an alliance which would probably involve them in a war with Russia, and consequently with France, in which they, as they firmly believed, would have to shoulder the principal burden.

I do not wish to omit, however, mentioning two other questions which came up in Balfour's and Chamberlain's talks with Bülow and the Kaiser. One concerned economic competition. Balfour, particularly, refused to admit that England was jealous of Germany's industrial progress; for England, he held, was so prosperous that she did not have to fear competition. The other question concerned the increase in the German fleet. At that time the second German Fleet Bill, which provided for a doubling of the German battleships, was already pending, and Bülow reported: 'The proposed strengthening of our fleet does not seem to be to Mr. Chamberlain's liking.' As a matter of fact, however, it does not appear that this question greatly influenced Chamberlain's attitude, nor that it particularly excited public opinion in England. Bülow's reserve, during his conversations with Chamberlain and Balfour, may perhaps be explained by the fact that he was convinced that Salisbury, while not exactly averse to meeting Germany's wishes, was not inclined to go as far as Chamberlain. And, finally, it may be permitted in this connexion to point to the extremely characteristic observations written down by Bülow on the occasion of his sojourn in England.

'The English politicians', one of the significant passages runs, 'know little about the Continent. They do not know much more about Continental conditions than we know about conditions in Peru and Siam. They are, moreover, according to our ideas, rather naïve both in their ingenuous egoism and in a certain kind of trustfulness. It is difficult for them to think that others have really *bad* intentions. They are quiet, phlegmatic, and optimistic. The South African situation excites people in Berlin more than it does political circles in England. One only hears it referred to when some relative has been wounded. Nobody has the least doubt that England will come well out of the affair. The country is solidly united in the opinion that the government must be supported until the situation in Africa is cleared up. If the government, after big British successes, should choke the throats of the Boers, even the most liberal Englishman would consider this to be quite in order. On the other hand, if the government, in case of further failures, and in order to avoid exaggerated sacrifices and expenses, should make a discreetly honourable peace with the South African Republics, even the Jingoes would not oppose such a policy. Everything is acceptable here which constitutes a practical solution. The land breathes wealth, self-satisfaction, contentment and confidence in its power and future. One notices that these people have never seen an enemy in their own country, and are incapable of believing that things could really ever go badly either at home or abroad. With the exception of a few leading men, they work very little and take their own time about everything. It is a physically and morally sound land. In general there is no question that the sentiment in England is much less anti-German than the feeling in Germany is anti-British. Therefore such Englishmen as Chirol and Saunders, who from personal experience know the acuteness and the depth of the German aversion against England, are the most dangerous. If the British public were really aware of the sentiment at present rife in Germany, it would cause a great change in their conception of the relations between the two countries.'

The conclusion which he reached was summed up as follows: 'I consider the future task of the German Government to be patiently and composedly to await further development of events, strong in the possession of a fleet which will protect German interests both against Russia and England.' The old formula—Time is with us, let us not be in a hurry—still prevailed. But Chamberlain was not to be put off. He, like many of his countrymen in those days, saw England's greatest adversary in a Russia capable of threatening India in the Far East. To compromise with Russia was, he believed, to court disaster. Therefore, he stuck to his plan of concluding an alliance with Germany and the United States. Soon after William the Second had left England for Germany, Chamberlain observed that the new Triple Alliance would, in a peaceful sense, overrun the world. But the Berlin Government was not inclined to co-operate. Bülow gave Chamberlain, as the latter remarked, 'the cold shoulder', and spoke in the Reichstag, in high sounding words, in favour of the Fleet Bill and of the desire for a Germany always ready on the high seas to resist any attack. As he expressed it: 'In the coming century, the German nation will be either hammer or anvil.' In addition he offended British sensibilities by abruptly demanding satisfaction for the seizure and search (without the knowledge of the British Government) of three German freight steamers, suspected of carrying contraband while they were en route to South Africa.

A suggestion emanating from St. Petersburg, that Germany should join Russia in a note addressed to England in favour of the Boers, was declined by Bülow, for he did not trust Russia or France and was afraid of being deserted by them

and left alone to face England. But the form of his refusal
was unfortunately chosen. Bülow told the Tsar that he
would have to leave the initiative in this matter to Russia.
He also emphasized the fact that Germany could only be
a party to such far-reaching schemes, if both Russia and
France would guarantee Germany's retention of her present
possessions for a great number of years. As might easily
have been conjectured, the Russian Minister for Foreign
Affairs, Muravieff, refused this advance with the declaration that a French Ministry which made such a pledge
could not last twenty-four hours; and France did not miss
the opportunity of reporting at once to London that
Germany had offered to act against England in the Boer
question in return for concessions. This was not strictly
true, but the incident naturally increased England's distrust and weakened the good impression which Germany's
strict neutrality in the course of the Boer war had hitherto
made in England. It is understandable, under these
circumstances, that the group of British ministers who had
favoured a connexion with Germany adopted for the time
being an attitude of reserve, a course which exactly suited
Bülow and Holstein, for both had remained unsympathetic to a firm alliance with England. They thought it
advisable that Germany should not be drawn into Anglo-
Russian controversies, and were convinced that, in preventing this, they were carrying out their master's axiom
that Germany must preserve her independence between
the two groups of Powers. They failed to realize that the
method which Bismarck had employed to achieve this
independence differed from theirs in important particulars.
True, Bismarck sought to keep the situation in hand as
long as possible, because a decision in favour of either
England or Russia would have given the French an ally,
the prevention of which was his leading motive (*Leitmotiv*).
But there can be no doubt that, if France had succeeded
in getting either the Russians or the British to form an

entente, he would have formed an alliance with the other Government, even before the re-grouping of the Powers could have taken effect, though it might have entailed heavy sacrifices. Bismarck had scented danger in every direction, and it was because he always keenly feared the formation of a coalition threatening Germany's existence that he was ever intent on extending his system of alliances and treaties.

His successors, however, trusting absolutely in Germany's military power, had permitted an alliance to be formed between Russia and France, and thought, in spite of the fact that this union grew closer and closer, that they could safeguard Germany's interests by adhering to the principle of the free hand. This is not the time or place in which to argue the question whether or not, as Bülow feared, an alliance with one of the two world powers—Russia or England—would in fact make the other Germany's deadly enemy. One thing, however, is certain, and that is that Germany's hesitation and her endeavours to maintain an attitude of independence towards both sides unfavourably prejudiced her position. This became very evident when Germany was forced to take a definite stand on the occasion of the Siberian conflicts in which England and Russia became embroiled in China in 1900. I am prevented by the shortness of the time at my disposal from describing these conflicts in detail. It must suffice to mention the fact that Russia sought to extend her authority in Manchuria, while England decided to use her influence in the Yangtse territory to exploit her commercial interests. Germany considered her task to be the safeguarding of the principle of the *open door* in favour of all commercially interested nations. That was made easier because of the parallel policy of the United States. But the desire of the German statesmen to be indulgent towards the interests of Russia in Manchuria as far as possible, without offending England, who saw herself threatened in this territory, gave rise to friction. It is true that in October, 1900, a treaty was concluded between England and Germany, but it contained the germs of new differences for the future and wrecked the new attempts made in 1901 for an Anglo-German agreement.

These attempts, as the British documents show, were not initiated by London, as was formerly supposed, but by Berlin. To what extent Eckardstein, who started these advances, was supported by the German Government is not possible to say with any degree of certainty. But it is clear that Chamberlain was glad to profit by the advance in order once more to bring under discussion his plan for a great world-power combination and to secure for himself a dependable ally, if the several conflicts in which England was at the time involved should compel her to take up arms. For England was still fighting against the Boers in South Africa, and her conflicts with Russia, both in Persia and China, continued. France was pushing herself forward in Morocco, and England's good relations with the United States suffered because of disputes over the control of the Panama Canal, which the United States were about to build. Chamberlain knew that the support of Germany could not be obtained without sacrifices, but he believed these sacrifices would be less than those necessary to effect an adjustment of all differences with Russia and France. Nor was he alone in this belief. The Duke of Devonshire was of the same opinion. Lansdowne, the Secretary of State for Foreign Affairs, was not as unconditionally in favour of Chamberlain's plans, as we formerly assumed from the German official documents, but it may well be that in private conversations he went somewhat further than his written declarations, to which we now have access, seem to indicate. The latter show that, from the beginning, he had doubts with regard to the German proposal in connexion with a defensive alliance, which would have obliged each of the two contracting parties to adopt armed intervention if the other should be attacked by two powers. It would be difficult, he added, to decide whether a nation was actually pursuing a defensive policy; the attacking country, as a matter of fact, might be apparently acting in self-defence against an attack which it had purposely provoked. Nor did Lansdowne omit to emphasize the difficulties which might confront England in consequence of such an alliance, particularly since Berlin now demanded that the alliance should be concluded not with Germany alone, but with the entire Triple Alliance.

Salisbury, from the very beginning, showed little interest in Chamberlain's plans. The older he grew, the more firmly he became rooted in the opinion that England could only rely on her fleet and her chalk cliffs. He held the same opinion as his son, Lord Cranborne: 'England does not solicit alliances, she grants them'; and he emphasized more pronouncedly the dangers of the far-reaching obligations which England would incur by the admission of Germany's allies into the alliance. Moreover, he doubted whether the isolation under which England, in the opinion of Germany, was supposed to be suffering, actually contained elements of danger. 'It would hardly be wise', he remarked, 'for us to enter upon burdensome obligations in order to protect ourselves from a danger which we do not believe to exist.' He pointed to the difficulties which would arise from merely *presenting* such an agreement with Germany to Parliament, and was of the opinion that England's attitude in a future crisis could never be foreseen; everything always depended upon the public opinion of the nation. Even more decided were the words of Sanderson, Permanent Under-Secretary of State for Foreign Affairs, who expressed the fear that it might be possible that Germany would be less scrupulous than England in carrying out the treaty—an accusation which was unfounded, but may be explained as born of the disagreements which arose over the interpretation of the Yangtse agreement concluded in October, 1900. Support against Russia in China was, as a matter of fact, one of the principal purposes underlying England's approach to Germany. The first article had laid down the principle of the open door in all Chinese territories as far as the influence of the contracting parties made it possible. This Germany interpreted to mean that intervention in Manchuria on her part could not at any time be requested by England. The second article of the treaty, however, guaranteed the maintenance, *without reservation*, of the territorial integrity of the Chinese Empire. When England, therefore, on the basis of this agreement, requested Germany to plead in St. Petersburg for China's inviolability, and thus protest against Russia's evident designs of annexation in Manchuria, Bülow declared that the Anglo-German agreement did not apply to Manchuria. 'I do not know', he said in the Reichstag, 'what could be of more indifference to us than the fate of Manchuria.' The indignation caused in England by this German interpretation of the Yangtse agreement was great. England saw in it a direct repudiation by Germany of the anti-Russian policy which at that time was still an axiom of many leading English politicians. The value of an alliance with Germany, therefore, declined in the eyes of British statesmen, and the favourable news from the South African war zone, as well as the decision to settle amicably the disagreements with the United States, increased the number of those who advised against the conclusion of a defensive alliance with Germany in the form demanded by the latter, because they considered this form opposed to the world interests of Great Britain. 'Treaty or no treaty', they said, 'should we ever face destruction, or only *defeat* by Russia and France, Germany would be compelled to assist us in order to avoid a similar fate. She might exact a high price for such help; but could that price be higher than that which we should pay by the sacrifice of our liberty to pursue a purely

British policy?' Shortly afterwards Bertie very justly remarked: 'Germany is in a precarious situation in Europe. She is surrounded by Governments which distrust her, and by nations who dislike her or at any rate bear her no love.'

In saying this he accurately summed up the situation according to which the attitude of the Emperor and the German statesmen must be judged. For was it not true that the world situation had so shaped itself that Germany was more in need of England's friendship than England was of hers? Were not men like Hatzfeldt, Metternich, and Eckardstein right in pointing out that a union with England was the only means of checking the dangers which threatened the German world policy? It may be permitted in this connexion to point to the excellent observations contained in a memorandum made by a high official of the German Foreign Office, Klehmet. In a very decided manner, he opposed the 'chauvinistic shouters' of the Pan-German circles, who had kindled the flame of anti-British sentiment, who urged the uncompromising assertion of German interests all over the world, and who demanded a fight to the finish with England. He reminded his readers of the fate of Spain and Portugal, who, by pressing their colonial plans too far, had courted disaster. He emphasized the possibility that England, repulsed by Germany, might straighten out her difficulties with Russia, and he energetically advocated the conclusion, as soon as possible, of a defensive alliance with England as the only means by which Germany would be able to thwart the menace of total isolation. His advice remained unheeded. William the Second, Bülow, and Holstein retained their opinion that Germany was in a favourable position to wait.

'Your Majesty', Bülow remarked at the beginning of the year, 'is quite right in feeling that the British must come to us. They have just lost a good deal of hair in Africa; America is uncertain; Japan is not to be depended upon; France is filled with hate; Russia is perfidious; public opinion is hostile in all countries. . . . At present it is beginning to dawn gradually on the minds of the British that they will not be able to hold their world Empire merely by their own power against so many opponents.'

The possibility that England and Russia, or England and France, might come to terms, they characterized as the outgrowth of a diseased fantasy. 'Time works for us', they repeated again and again. 'Only if the British pledge themselves, body and soul, to the Triple Alliance, can we give up the policy of the free hand.' 'All or nothing'— these words characterized their attitude. In this sense, they demanded that their allies should be included in the treaty, advised negotiations between England and Austria-Hungary, and suggested the adherence to the treaty not only of Japan but possibly also of Turkey and Rumania. With this requirement Chamberlain's efforts, which had lasted three years, were doomed. Salisbury had won; his conviction that an alliance with Germany was no life and death matter to his country, and ought not to be purchased at too high a sacrifice, had carried the day. But the desire to await the success of the negotiations already begun for an alliance with Japan may have prompted the British statesmen not to break off abruptly with Germany, and once more to attempt to come to an understanding on special questions. The Moroccan question, in which the interests of England and France conflicted, offered a chance to renew exchanges of opinion. But again the German statesmen's distrust of the sincerity of British policy wrecked all efforts to come to an understanding. Equally unsuccessful was a conversation between the Kaiser and the British Ambassador, Lascelles. Towards the end of the year, when the negotiations with Japan were approaching a favourable conclusion, and the complete defeat of the Boers was expected with certainty, the definite refusal of England to enter into an alliance with Germany was announced. Chamberlain was sorely disappointed by his failure, and indignant at the tone adopted against him and the British nation by public opinion in Germany. He opened his heart to the Austro-Hungarian Ambassador. For years, he declared, he had been of the opinion that England should join the Triple Alliance. He had always worked for this idea and made use of every opportunity to realize it. Two years ago, when Count Bülow accompanied the Kaiser to Windsor, he (Chamberlain) had discussed the various questions of foreign policy with the former and had convinced himself that, in the majority of questions, England and Germany had the same interests, and that, therefore, a co-operation with the Triple Alliance was just as much in the interest of England as in that of the Triple Alliance itself. 'For that very reason', he said, 'an agreement which would have been favourable to both parties did not appear impossible of achievement, although I never underestimated the great difficulties ahead of me, because I well realized that such an agreement was contrary to English tradition. I will not maintain that I could have achieved that goal; but, after the fierce attacks and abuse to which England has been subjected by Germany for the last few weeks, a realization of these projects is now out of the question.' He did not wish to have anything more to do with Bülow. As late as July, 1905, he said to Mensdorff: 'Once burned, twice shy; from that moment I was determined never again to run in double harness with that man.'

In Berlin, however, the news of the failure of the negotiations was hailed with exultation by the Pan-Germans, with a certain amount of satisfaction by Bülow and Holstein, and with indifference by the majority of the politicians. Had they not succeeded in retaining their liberty? Had they not avoided being taken in tow by British policy? Were they not now in a position to wait? 'The British difficulties will increase still further, and with them the price which we demand', observed Bülow. An impartial

and just opinion, however, will admit that the leading
German statesmen had made an irreparable mistake when
they refused to take the outstretched hand of England.
Again these statesmen had forgotten the doctrine of their
teacher Bismarck: 'An alliance', he had said, 'should not
be entered into with a proclamation that one is ready to go
through thick and thin for an ally. An alliance can only be
formed by common policy, especially in the case of a
country whose foreign policy changes with changes in the
Ministry.' That the German statesmen declined a defensive alliance, as limited by the demands of England, may
readily be understood; but they cannot be excused for
declining the proposals of agreement on single questions
which would have tended to strengthen the mutual confidence of the two nations. Thus an Anglo-German entente
might have been formed which would have constituted the
basis for a future alliance. By their rigid insistence upon the
principle of 'all or nothing', the German statesmen missed
the opportunity to enter into a union which would have
proved of advantage to Germany and perhaps beneficial
to the entire world. They also diverted the British statesmen into a path which, in the course of time, led to the conclusion of the *entente* with France and Russia. The word
of the poet cited by Bülow: 'Was man von der Minute
ausgeschlagen, gibt keine Ewigkeit zurück' (What thou
hast rejected in a moment of time, eternity cannot restore),
cannot be applied more aptly to any one than to Bülow
himself and to his associates.

England, after Germany's refusal, had to look out for
another ally upon whom she could rely in the event of a
war against Russia. For Russia was still considered the
arch-enemy by practically all classes in the nation, and
also by the great majority of the leading statesmen, although certain voices, on account of Germany's attitude,
began to advocate coming to an understanding with
Russia. Russia had just turned all her attention to the

Far East and attempted to widen her domination in Manchuria and increase her influence in China; and there was a danger that, by an advance in Persia and Tibet, she might menace the British rule in India. Japan, threatened even more directly by Russia, presented herself as a logical ally. At the time when the success of the Anglo-German negotiations was believed possible, the plan of inviting Japan to join the alliance had been considered and the discussions with the able Ambassador of Japan at London, Baron Hayashi, made it evident that he was well disposed to seize this opportunity to benefit his country. After the miscarriage of the proposed Anglo-German alliance, the negotiations were continued with Japan by the British statesmen; and, after bridging over many difficulties—for a very strong party in Japan was working for a smoothing over of the difficulties with Russia—a treaty of alliance was finally signed on January 30, 1902. The two Powers undertook to adopt common measures to protect their interests in the Far East in the event of an aggressive advance by any other power, and to maintain the independence and integrity of China and Korea. Should England or Japan, in the course of events, go to war with any power which threatened her interests, her ally undertook to preserve a benevolent neutrality. But should the aggressor—and here the allies had Russia in mind—be supported by some other power—and this could, in the existing circumstances, be France only—the ally not directly attacked was pledged to armed assistance. These were, as may readily be seen, practically the same principles which guided the British statesmen in their negotiations with Germany. The Swedish scholar, Kjellén, has aptly said that it was very significant that the Anglo-Japanese alliance had arisen out of the abortive attempts to procure an understanding between England and Germany, on the one hand, and between Russia and Japan on the other. The extraordinary significance of the

Anglo-Japanese alliance for world politics lay in the fact that with its conclusion England ceased to follow the policy of splendid isolation which had been her course for so many years. She was led to give up this policy by the realization that she could not be mistress of the seas unless she had strong allies. These she sought, as she had in the eighteenth century; but instead of a Continental, she now sought an extra-European power. The alliance was unwelcome to Russia and France, and the former attempted to win over Germany to renew the East-Asiatic alliance of 1895; and on this occasion, certain words were spoken which tended to revive the idea of the possibility of a Continental alliance against England. But Germany declined, with the explanation that such an alliance would jeopardize her Japanese market, while England and Japan might be prompted to unite with the United States. Russia and France now agreed to extend their alliance to Eastern Asia. Germany was informed of the conclusion of the Anglo-Japanese alliance, but was not invited to become a member of it, and indeed neither the Kaiser nor Bülow would have had any inclination to accept an invitation which they had refused in the past. To remain free, without tying themselves down to any side, remained, as formerly, their watchword in reference to this question. A little later Bülow said: 'For me it is, and always will be, a fundamental principle of German diplomacy, that we have no Oriental policy and that we are the catspaw for no one in the world.' And the Kaiser agreed. This, in the abstract, was a correct opinion, but the question was whether or not Germany was in a position to rely on her own strength in competing for world power. The great significance of England's estrangement from Germany does not seem to have been clearly realized at first by the leaders of Germany's foreign policy. They could not give up the idea that the enmity between England and Russia, rivals in the East, would continue to endure. At the same time, relations between St. Petersburg and Berlin were becoming ever more friendly, and the German statesmen believed that the way would always be open for them to make an agreement with Russia, although the Franco-Russian alliance was growing stronger all the time, and there was a strong active anti-German party in Russia. This again clearly shows the difference between the statesmanship of Bismarck and his successors. Bismarck always kept in mind the possibility of even the most improbable coalitions and sought to hold a counter-alliance in readiness as a trump card. But the Kaiser, Bülow, and Holstein at that time did not think of the possibility of any such anti-German coalition, and therefore did not take one into account. For them there was first a Dual Alliance—France and Russia—in whose eventual aggression they believed. They considered, however, that the Triple Alliance—which was renewed in 1902—was strong enough to repulse their attack. Secondly, there was England, with whom the German statesmen were quite willing to be friendly, provided Germany did not have to make any sacrifice contrary to her future interests. There was only one question: whether the British statesmen would be disposed to regard the expansion of the German Empire with composure, or whether they would ally with their former opponents, France and Russia—as they had frequently threatened to do—in order with united strength to counteract Germany's efforts to extend her world power. That they did so, and how, will be the subject of my next lecture.

LECTURE V
(1902–1908)

AS victors over the Boers and as Japan's ally, England
could devote herself more freely and with more confidence to the diplomatic struggle against her rivals and
enemies. I should like to emphasize again that then, as
later in their diplomatic warfare, the efforts of the leading
British statesmen were directed towards the prevention,
if it were at all possible, of war, even with Russia; since,
although it was in England's interest to weaken Russia in
the Far East, especially as long as the differences between
England and France had not been overcome, it was not in
her interest to encompass Russia's downfall. For the ruin
of Russia must bring in its train an extension of German
power that could not be other than unwelcome to England
in view of the failure of the attempt to achieve an understanding with Germany, whose rapidly increasing naval
armaments and participation in the construction of strategic
railways in Asia Minor menaced the British Empire.
England, therefore, mapped out her policy with the following considerations in view. It was necessary, first of all, to
win France; then to hold Russia in check by means of
Japan; to be in friendly agreement with Italy; and to let
Germany feel England's strength, in order to induce her to
desist from increasing her fleet with a rapidity dangerous
to British sea-power, and from threatening England's interests in the different parts of the world.

British statesmen did not imagine that a compromise
with France was to be obtained easily and without sacrifices. No nation had more vehemently taken the part of
the Boers than had the French; the Fashoda affair was not
forgotten; nor was French public opinion then favourable
to England. But what made the agreement between the
two Governments so difficult to obtain was not so much the
seriousness of the controversies as the large number of points

over which controversies could arise. The interests of the
two crossed in Abyssinia, Senegambia, Uganda, and in
Madagascar; in Newfoundland, and in Siam, and in the
New Hebrides. But the most important cause of friction between the two countries was Egypt, where the still legally
existing treaty with France hampered England in the
exercise of her authority. To all these points of controversy
had been added Morocco, where France had acquired great
influence during the Boer war, and where her position had
been made still more powerful by the treaty concluded with
the Sultan of Morocco in 1900. Nor did France remain
satisfied with what she had acquired; she was bending her
efforts towards securing a share of Morocco. She singled out
Spain as an ally, intending to make her a grant of a small
part of Morocco, and entered into an agreement with
Italy, with whom her relations had become more close in
the course of the years 1898–1901, by which France was
assured of a free hand in Morocco in return for her support
of Italian pretensions in Tripoli. We have already learnt
of the anxiety caused in London by this policy on the part
of France and of the large part played by the Moroccan
question in the negotiations between Germany and
England. The French possession of Tangier would be a
constant danger to the entry of the British Fleet into the
Mediterranean. That France's action had been taken
without consideration for England at the time of the Boer
war gave rise to much bitterness in London and caused
England, after her victory in South Africa, to denounce
France and to prevail upon Spain, just then experiencing
a change of ministry, to abandon the plan of treating with
France. The result was a deepening of the already existing
gulf between the two nations. As early as September, 1902,
in reply to Mensdorff's query as to whether negotiations
for an understanding between England and France were
in progress, Bertie said: 'The old game begins anew. France
wants to play England off against Germany, and Germany

England against France. Both seek to sow discord.' In his opinion it would be a great mistake on England's part to allow herself to be drawn towards either side. England was far stronger when she kept aloof from all alliances, and the cause of European peace was better served when neither group was strengthened by the addition of British power.

Nevertheless, the British statesmen—above all Lansdowne—grasped the hand of reconciliation held out to them by the outspokenly anglophile and germanophobe French Foreign Minister, Delcassé. As always when expediency advised it, they knew how to let bygones be bygones. To-day the publication of the British diplomatic documents enables us to follow the long negotiations and watch the manner in which the end was attained. With considerable cleverness the British set to work to open up channels for friendly relations with France, relations which formed the indispensable hypothesis for the favourable solution of controversial questions. King Edward took on himself the task of paving the way towards an understanding with France and did splendid work. The part played by King Edward in these negotiations, as indeed his influence upon the conduct of affairs throughout his reign, has been greatly overestimated on the Continent, and especially in Germany. With great truth Mensdorff observed some years later that King Edward had been so overpraised that he was made to appear as the protagonist in the foreign policy of his reign. In accomplishing a better mutual understanding between England and France, he was aided by the fact that Delcassé met him half way. He who, as we have already heard, had been instrumental in promoting the *rapprochement* between France and Italy, was now the most insistent advocate of an Anglo-French *entente*. In November, 1903, Mensdorff reported: 'The majority of Englishmen to-day desire to live with France in peace and friendship. A warm sympathy exists for

France.' And Bertie said to him: 'For us France is more important than Germany or Russia or any other Power. If we are certain of France, no one can have designs upon us.'

That the negotiations carried on between the cabinets of Paris and London resulted finally in a treaty, which was relatively favourable to England, was due, in the first place, to the fact that in February, 1904, the Russo-Japanese war broke out and was followed almost immediately by the decisive defeat of Russia in Manchuria. France saw with alarm the collapse of her ally. Thus it came about that on April 8, 1904, at a time advantageous to England, the Anglo-French treaty was concluded. England's rule in Egypt, contested by France since 1882, was recognized; permission was given to France to establish herself in Morocco. Spain, as well as France, was given the opportunity to extend her sphere of power and influence there. So England benefited immediately by the treaty, whereas France would benefit only after much labour in Morocco. The two Powers also came to terms over a large number of controversial questions, in all parts of the world other than Europe. The observation of a strict neutrality in the war between Russia and Japan was, indeed, not expressly mentioned, but tacitly implied. Above all, the two Powers pledged themselves to mutual diplomatic support in conflicts with other Powers that might arise out of their agreements over Egypt and Morocco; and in this agreement lay the international historical importance of the then concluded treaties by which the two Powers, who for so long had been warring with each other, composed their differences and successfully settled all critical questions. The arrangement was not an actual alliance, but an understanding of so broad a nature that co-operation would develop naturally, should questions of world-wide importance arise.

And this treaty was a turning-point, not alone in Anglo-French relations but in Anglo-German and Franco-

German relations also. For Morocco was also a subject of conflict between France and Germany. The concession which England made to France in Morocco contradicted the international treaty of Madrid, 1880, to which the two Powers had also been signatories, whereby a protectorate of a kind such as France was now encouraged to undertake had been prohibited. In the same contradiction were the two Franco-Spanish treaties concluded in October, 1904, as a result of the Anglo-French *Entente Cordiale*. The four treaties created a system, complete in itself, for the purpose of establishing the French protectorate in Morocco.

In general, the Anglo-French treaty should have shown Germany that the time was now past when, protected by the enmity between England and Russia and the rivalry between England and France, she could hope to be able to develop her plans of 'Weltpolitik'. In certain aspects the situation in which William II and his advisers found themselves after the conclusion of the Anglo-French *Entente* resembles that in which Frederick II of Prussia found himself in 1756. Frederick had not thought it possible that the old adversaries, Austria and France, could become reconciled to each other and make war upon him. William II and his advisers believed as little that England and France could settle their numerous disputes. Frederick II, however, at once grasped the situation and made certain of a valuable compensation in England for the disloyalty of France. William II and his advisers, on the contrary, underestimated the change that had come about in the grouping of the European Powers, and continued to believe that they could still choose as they liked between the East and the West. For they were firmly convinced that an Anglo-Russian agreement lay outside the bounds of possibility, and that consequently Germany would remain free in case of necessity to conclude an alliance with her powerful neighbour in the East. The French

politicians chose another and more far-sighted policy.
Just as Bismarck had once devoted all his energy to isolat-
ing France, and thereby preventing the outbreak of a war
of revenge, so now the French were busy effecting the
isolation of Germany and securing allies for themselves
against the coming of the day of reckoning for the wrong
they believed themselves to have suffered. The first step
was the alliance with Russia; the second the *rapprochement*
with Italy during the years 1898–1902; and the *Entente
Cordiale* was the third. In the succeeding years they advanced still further along this road. France, and not
England, as is always said even in Germany, initiated all
the agreements by which Germany was isolated and which
resulted in that situation known in Germany as the
'Einkreisung', or encirclement. Not only did the French
statesmen induce a not infrequently unwilling Russia to
agree to the extension of the political alliance and military
conventions of 1891–4, but they also worked in England
with tireless energy for the deepening and broadening of
the alliance of which the foundation had been laid in the
Entente Cordiale of 1904. Moreover, they excelled the
German politicians of their day in their refusal to lay, as
did the Germans, the chief emphasis upon the drafting of
a far-reaching treaty of alliance. Unlike the Germans, who
were worshippers of the phrase 'all or nothing', the French
placed the greatest value upon practical co-operation.

The treaties of 1904 meant the end of a lengthy period
of peace assured. Since the crises during the period 1887
to 1890, war had never seriously threatened the Continental Great Powers. After 1904, not one year passed
without a direct threat of war. As each came to naught,
there was a sigh of relief, but one threat followed the
other in orderly succession, and hung 'like thunder-
clouds over Europe, until the outbreak of the long-dreaded
World War'.

The news of the conclusion of the Anglo-French treaty

was received in Germany not without uneasiness. The Kaiser in particular saw in this agreement a success for France in that she had won England's friendship without sacrificing that of Russia. He was not slow in recognizing the danger in the fact that England could now pay less regard to Germany, but Bülow quieted his fears by insinuating that the varying interests of France and England in the Far East rendered a lasting friendship impossible. England would be compelled to support Japan, while France must support Russia. Holstein was also never tired of declaring that the time had not yet come to sacrifice oneself for the sake of a foreign Power, that Germany still remained the indicator in the balance, and that her arbitral position should not be surrendered. His point of view was modified by Germany's attitude during the first months of the Russo-Japanese war. She preserved her neutrality, but lent Russia (the Kaiser's decided aversion to the yellow race contributed to this), as far as the limits of her own neutrality would allow, her diplomatic and commercial support, and made it possible for Russia to uncover her western boundaries. England was displeased by the Russophil attitude of Germany, and she protested against Germany supplying coal by indirect means to the Russian fleet. The Dogger Bank Incident in 1904—and the rumour that immediately ran through England that Germany was indirectly responsible for this incident—increased the bad feeling between the countries. It was openly said that Germany must be held in check and a further increase in her naval armaments forbidden, since she undoubtedly intended to fight England. Balfour told Mensdorff at this time that public opinion in England was just as stupid as in Germany. 'I think', he said, 'that the distrust of the German leaders is unfounded, and that it is wrong to ascribe to them aggressive or Machiavellian plans. But they have shown themselves very stupid in recent years. What bad diplomats they are!'.

Such declarations had their echo in Germany, and the Anglophobe sentiments of wide circles in German society did not fail to influence the rulers of the nation.

An attempt was made at that time on the part of Germany to separate Russia from France, or through Russian influence over France to gain the latter Power for the old idea of a Continental Alliance. Holstein was particularly active in pursuit of this aim and the Kaiser willingly followed his lead. The attempt to effect an agreement on this basis broke down in the face of the opposition of the Russian ministers, who knew how to convince the Tsar, at first in favour of the scheme, that care must be taken not to put France in such a situation as would compel her to enter unwillingly into an agreement of which she (France) disapproved, or which would necessitate her loosening the bonds that bound her to Russia and entering into still closer relations with England, the ally of Russia's enemy, Japan.

Russia's reserve vexed Germany all the more, since her relations with the Western European Great Powers were growing obviously worse from month to month. At the end of 1904, England announced an increase in her navy, which showed clearly that the British Admiralty held the regrouping of naval strength to be a necessity; soon after, the building of dreadnoughts was begun in order to offset the German fleet in armament as well as in numerical strength. At the same time, Germany's interests in Morocco were being threatened by France, who was endeavouring to establish her protectorate there by means of so-called peaceful penetration. Large sections of the German people—the Pan-Germans, who were growing in influence, in particular —wished to combat these inimical pursuits by taking energetic steps against them, and called upon the Government to take the necessary measures. The Emperor William disliked the idea of taking such steps, and especially desired at this time to avoid a conflict with France in

view of the situation in Morocco, but he allowed himself
to be persuaded by Bülow, behind whom Holstein as the
real instigator lay hidden, to call at Tangier on his
Mediterranean cruise. He declared himself, in a speech
he made in Tangier (March 31, 1905), to be a supporter of
the sovereignty of the Sultan of Morocco, and at the same
time he let it be known that Germany would insist upon
the satisfaction of her rightful claims in Morocco. The
Emperor's speech caused astonishment and anxiety in
London and Paris, and it was believed that Germany
intended to take the opportunity afforded her by Russia's
defeat in the war with Japan in order to embark upon a
war to the death against France. Delcassé turned to the
British Government in the hope of being able to assure
himself of England's support in the event of war. The
British diplomatic documents reveal that the British
Government never thought of concluding an alliance with
France. Lansdowne stated that he was only prepared to
lend his support to France in her determined opposition to
the acquisition by Germany of a port on the coast of
Morocco, and he invited France to join with him in discussing the dangers that could arise out of such a policy. He
told the German Ambassador that public opinion was such
as to compel the Government in case of necessity to adopt
energetic measures in the event of France being attacked.
From this statement and from those of very highly-placed
Englishmen, Delcassé may have formed his belief that he
could hope for the armed support of England, and in this
conviction he refused the German proposal for a conference of the Powers signatories to the Madrid Agreement
for the purpose of solving the Moroccan question. In so
doing he knew he incurred the danger of war. Nevertheless he must certainly have calculated that England could
not undisturbedly watch the destruction of France and
that, although reluctantly, she would be forced by public
opinion to take her stand by the side of Germany's

enemies. This belief was shared by Metternich, German Ambassador at London, who warned his Government by declaring that 'there can be no doubt that England will stand unconditionally and actively on the French side and go against Germany, even with enthusiasm'.

Delcassé's ministerial colleagues, and above all the Prime Minister Rouvier, did not believe that they could risk a war against Germany under such circumstances, especially as the Minister of War pronounced the chances of victory to be very doubtful and the assistance of England, if forthcoming, as insufficient. Delcassé resigned, and his successor accepted the conference proposed by Germany. The British Government, which had for a long time opposed the holding of a conference, also finally abandoned their resistance. But if Germany had gained her object, she was required to pay dearly for her triumph. The current of anti-German feeling in England ran high; a large number of British newspapers and reviews vied with each other in invective against William II and the German Government. This being the position, it is plain that Germany's relations with Russia were of the greatest importance to her destiny. The Emperor William became more and more strongly convinced that the time had come to make an end of the continued indecision, and that he ran the risk, by hesitating any longer, of falling between two stools. For this reason, at the very moment when the Moroccan crisis reached its height, and a wave of dislike for England was sweeping over the Empire, the Emperor decided to renew the attempt which had failed in the previous year to achieve an alliance with Russia. The Tsar had been defeated, and found himself in a very disagreeable situation. He hated King Edward, whom he described, in his private letters to William (though we must allow for his wish to please the recipient), as 'the arch-intriguer and disturber of the peace'. The Kaiser he styled his 'sincere friend'. The hostility between Austria-Hungary and Russia was now no longer such an obstacle to a Russo-German alliance as it had been in former decades. The deeply-rooted differences between Austria-Hungary and Russia, keen rivals in the Balkans, had not, it is true, been removed, yet a certain *rapprochement* had taken place between them by the Mürzsteg Convention in the autumn of 1903. And a year later Francis Joseph showed how important he thought the maintenance of friendly relations with Russia by concluding a treaty of neutrality and by the sincerely meant and faithfully fulfilled pledge not to take advantage of Russia's conflicts in the Far East by making a sudden attack in the Balkans. 'For a moment the ghost of Bismarck's great creation, the League of the Three Emperors, hovered above the horizon; then disappeared again—for ever.'

In June, 1905, William and Nicholas met at Björkö in the Finnish islands. Here the Kaiser was successful in obtaining the Tsar's signature to a treaty which pledged each power to military assistance in *Europe*, in case of attack on the other. At the same time it was laid down that on the ratification of the treaty France should be informed of its content by Russia and invited to become a party to it. It was the old and cherished plan of William, the plan of a Continental alliance that would undoubtedly be directed against England, which the Emperor, after the unsuccessful attempt of the previous year, once again and this time with apparent success, put forward. William triumphed. In his confidential correspondence with Nicholas II the very excitable Kaiser denoted as the purpose of the treaty, 'the cooling of England's arrogance and impertinence'. 'The 24th July, 1905', runs his letter of July 27, 'is a corner-stone in European politics and turns over a new leaf in the history of the world, which will be a chapter of peace and goodwill among the Great Powers of the European Continent respecting each other in friendship, confidence, and in pursuing a general policy on the

lines of a community of interests.' The final words left
no doubt that the alliance was intended to be used against
England. But William's dream was not fulfilled. The
realization of this alliance, so eagerly sought by him, was
frustrated by the opposition of the German and Russian
ministers for foreign affairs. Bülow was of the opinion that
the alliance would have no significance if Russia was
pledged to give assistance in *Europe only* in a war between
Germany and England. The Russian minister maintained
that if the Tsar entered into an alliance of that sort with
Germany, he would be breaking faith with France; and
France's entry into the alliance would be impossible to
secure. Nicholas II could not deny that his minister was
justified in his opinion; and since, removed from the
Kaiser's personal influence, the Tsar believed he must
acquiesce in his minister's verdict, he shuffled off the engagement. Therewith the plan, mooted now by Germany,
now by Russia, of a great Continental alliance against
England was finally shattered, a plan that from its inception no serious German statesman can have believed
possible of realization. The conduct of William and
his advisers strengthened the anti-German feeling in
England—a feeling that found expression in the Press.
England did not ignore the warning provided by the
interview between the two Emperors. She sent the
British fleet to the Baltic in order to show Germany as
well as Russia that she was mistress of the Baltic as well as
of the other seas. In 1905, she strengthened her position
also in the Far East, by renewing and extending the treaty
she had made with Japan in 1902. This treaty placed
India under the protection of both allies, England and
Japan, and emphasized that each ally was under obligation to give armed assistance in the event of the other being
menaced by *one* Great Power—not, as in the treaty of 1902,
only if menaced by more than one.

Shortly afterwards a further important step was taken.

On the initiative of the French, conversations had taken place already, during Lansdowne's tenure of the Foreign Office, between the French and British naval staffs with regard to the redistribution of the British naval forces and the danger of a war with Germany. Shortly afterwards, when Grey took over the Foreign Office in succession to Lansdowne, the French Ambassador, Paul Cambon, on the eve of the Algeciras Conference, inquired whether England would undertake to give France military support in the event of an unprovoked German attack upon France. To-day we know that Grey refused to give a binding promise, but at the same time he communicated his belief to Metternich and Cambon that in event of an unprovoked attack by Germany upon France public opinion in England would demand intervention. Immediately afterwards official conversations took place between the French and British staffs that led to an agreement for the defence of either of the two Powers against the danger that might threaten her. The British documents reveal that it was definitely stated on the part of England that the agreement could in no way be regarded as curbing the liberty of decision of the British Government in the event of the question of intervention becoming acute. In effect, however, France—to paraphrase Goethe's words—'out of all heard only the "yes" '. According to Grey, who gives expression to these discussions in his Memoirs, it was impossible to refuse to take part in the military 'conversations', as he styles these negotiations, since to do so would have brought about a breach in the Anglo-French *Entente*, which he held to be vital for England's interests. Sense of duty to make preparations to counter presumed aggressive plans of Germany, and not any desire for offensive designs, which then as subsequently was foreign to British statesmen, compelled them to give their assent to the conversations held in 1906 between the British and Belgian staffs for the purpose of drawing up measures to defend Belgium against invasion.

The effect of the tension between England and Germany was also shown in the course of the Algeciras Conference of 1906, in which England took her stand by France in all decisive questions, and materially contributed to compel Germany to content herself with the independence of the Sultan of Morocco and the inviolability of his territories, whilst France gained her ends in the really critical questions—i.e. police reform and finance administration. The German Moroccan policy, which was inspired by Bülow, Holstein, and the Pan-Germans, was unwillingly assented to by the Emperor and was severely condemned by many German politicians. Bülow sought to defend it by asserting that the rapid increase in population, the growth in German industries, and the commercial proficiency of the German people had made necessary Germany's participation in world politics and the protection of her overseas interests. The accuracy of this statement cannot be denied; but it must be admitted that he and his advisers gave no proof of diplomatic skill in taking a stand in opposition to the rest of the Great Powers, especially a stand in opposition to England, without being certain of the support of one Great Power other than Austria-Hungary.

Everything that had happened since that day on which German statesmen, in ignorance of the true situation, had repulsed the hand held out to them by England must have forced them to realize that their policy did not agree with the true interests of Germany. The two alliances with Japan, the *Entente* with France, the improved relations with the United States, all served to show that England was well on the way to regain her long threatened position. Clever politicians knew that the notion of an unbridgeable gulf between Russia and England was a false one. From the recently published British diplomatic documents one realizes now that it was at least questionable whether England could have been induced to enter into a similar agreement with Germany after she had concluded the *Entente Cordiale* with France. Crowe, Hardinge, and Grey were against such a policy, while Bertie—at a time when the German Press was urging that England should be called upon to assist in restoring better relations between France and Germany—declared that England dare not do anything 'to facilitate an understanding between Germany and France; for it is difficult to conceive how an understanding of any real importance between these two countries could be satisfactory to Germany, without being detrimental to our interests'. All this does not mean, however, that England was not ready to establish friendly relations with Germany, provided that the latter did not ask too great a price for her friendship, and provided that Germany adopted a less expansive naval and commercial policy. Nothing could be of greater danger to Germany herself than the notion that had entered into many minds in Europe that she could make use of her economic and military power, which grew steadily from year to year, to disturb the balance of power and threaten the freedom of Europe. The Treaty of Björkö and the Kaiser's attempt to league the Continent against England could not fail to strengthen this anxiety.

The task of clever German statesmanship would have been to allay this fear, and to convince Europe that all such plans were far from the thought of the Emperor and his advisers—as was in truth the case—and that the maintenance of peace lay in Germany's own interest, considering how powerful the German nation had become in times of peace. Moreover, British public opinion was to be convinced that England could expect from Germany assistance and not opposition in the pursuit of her vital interests, and that Germany would ask no price from England for her co-operation that England could not pay with perfect safety to her position as a Great Power.

Instead of pursuing such a policy, however, the Kaiser determined to irritate England in the very place in which she was most sensitive—the defence of her lordship of the seas.

If we wish to judge British policy fairly in this question, we must not forget that England had cause for grave apprehension. Up to 1870, England as sea-power had been stronger, not only than any other single sea-power, but stronger also than any possible alliance of European sea-powers. That time was now past. Rivals had appeared, and in the last two decades she had had to consider the possible alliance against her of the fleets of France and Russia, these being *next* to her own in strength. Bearing this danger in mind, England had concluded in 1887 the treaties to which we have already referred with Italy and Austria-Hungary, in order that she might be able to count upon their support in defending the Suez Canal and Constantinople. Since the beginning of the twentieth century, the building of large warships by two other Great Powers—Germany and the United States—had further altered the situation. Japan, Italy, and Austria-Hungary followed in their lead. England's naval supremacy was in danger of being questioned. This fact, as we have seen, forced her to emerge from her aloofness and to seek for allies to assist her in maintaining her position as mistress of the seas. The two treaties with Japan assured her of Japanese assistance, and the *Entente Cordiale* of that of France. A war with the United States had become virtually unthinkable, and the destruction of the Russian fleet at Tsushima had released England from the fear of one day seeing the supposedly strong Russian fleet fighting on the side of her enemies. Germany was thus the only Power from whom she anticipated danger, and Germany was continuing the building of her fleet undeterred by British remonstrances.

The first two German Navy Bills did not arouse much anxiety in England, and, as far as it is possible to judge, they played no part in the negotiations for an alliance that filled the years 1898–1901. No request was proffered by England for a reduction in the German naval programme or a delay in its execution. It was not until the failure of these negotiations that there began a daily campaign in the anti-German British Press to warn public opinion and military circles of the danger threatening England from the growth of the German Navy, and to demand that the Government should take measures to protect the country against this danger. As a result the distribution of the British fleet was altered during the years 1903–6. The great majority of British warships were removed from the Mediterranean on the conclusion of the *Entente Cordiale*. After the destruction of the Russian fleet at the hands of Japan a similar movement homewards of British vessels took place in the waters of the Far East. The Channel fleet was strengthened; a great naval base was constructed at Rosyth; and the formation of a Home fleet in the North Sea was planned. Yet these preparations were certainly not being made with the object of attacking Germany—this the German Ambassador at London, Count Metternich, had invariably declared in the most emphatic manner to his Government. Nevertheless, in Germany British newspapers were being read in which the question was asked whether England should not anticipate matters and destroy the German fleet while such a task was still an easy one. Attention was paid to a speech of the First Lord of the Admiralty, Lord Lee, in which he declared that 'the Germans ought to be forbidden any further development of their fleet, but if the war came about in spite of all, the German fleet would be destroyed before Germany had time to read the declaration of war in the newspapers'. Speeches like this and other similar utterances aroused Germany. Lord Rosebery said of Lee's speech to Mensdorff: 'If a man finds himself in the same room with a German, and sneezes, the German raises a

storm and says that he has come too near to him.' But
anti-British circles in Germany made use of these out-
bursts to argue that Germany was in danger of being
attacked and that the necessity of taking measures for her
defence was urgent. England's policy before and during
the Algeciras Conference poured oil upon their fire. The
opinion steadily grew in influential circles that England
was not averse to the outbreak of a Franco-German war,
and that she would not permit Germany to emerge the
victor. A victory for Germany would in British eyes—so
the new Chief of the German General Staff, von Moltke,
declared in February, 1906—lead to a permanent occupation of Belgium and the Flanders coast by Germany, and
to the annexation of Holland in some form that would
seriously inconvenience British commerce and greatly
increase the danger of an invasion of England. It is,
indeed, certain that the fear of an invasion on the part
of Germany was groundless: an attempted invasion by
Germany would have been absurd. What is certain is
that the German Navy was regarded in Germany only as
a defensive arm, as a weapon for use against an attack of
England, but in England fears were entertained that it
might be used in an attack upon the British Isles. Thus
the anger in England can easily be understood at the
introduction of a new Navy Bill in the Reichstag by
Admiral von Tirpitz, who was the cleverest and most
energetic supporter of the Kaiser's naval plans, by which
it was proposed not only to increase the actual building
programme of the German Navy by the addition before
1917 of six great cruisers, but also to increase the size and
armament of all battleships already in course of construction or to be built in the future. The Bill became law in
May, 1906, and the construction of the German dreadnoughts was commenced forthwith. Only two courses now
remained open by which England, in the belief that she
must at all costs retain her naval supremacy, could counter

the German naval programme. Germany must slow down, or reduce, her naval armaments; or England must speed up and enlarge her own naval programme to an extent that would enable her to retain her superiority in the future.

British statesmen made many attempts to attain their end by trying to induce Germany to adopt the first course. Haldane, the War Minister, and Grey were especially active in this sense. Haldane declared to Mensdorff in July, 1906, that the British Government were ready to reduce their own naval programme if Germany would voluntarily do the same. In this case England would work also to accomplish a reduction in French armaments. They were prepared to tell the French—Haldane said—that they would not 'permit Germany to embark on a war of aggression against France. At the same time we will not support France if the agitation in France to bring about a war of revenge to win back Alsace-Lorraine gains the day'. Haldane often said to Grey: 'You understand the French, and therefore you deal with them. Leave the Germans to me: for I understand them. I am not unfamiliar with the famous tactlessness of the Prussians.' He knew that it could be handled and that too great importance should not be attached to it. Grey used the same language as Haldane to Mensdorff. England, Germany, and France—he told the Austrian Ambassador —must make a first step towards the abandonment of these vast naval and military armaments. The first thing to be done was to bring about a more or less stationary state of affairs: no great new naval programme and no increase in the strengths of the armies. Nevertheless, all efforts on the part of England's leading statesmen, who would have preferred this solution to induce Germany to reduce her naval programme remained unsuccessful. The Peace Conference at the Hague in 1907 separated without having earnestly discussed the motion brought forward by England for a limitation in armaments. Thus British statesmen found themselves compelled to adopt the second course: that of increasing the British Navy. The burdens that this involved for the British people contributed to heighten the dislike of the nation for the cause of all their troubles, and to strengthen them in their belief that Germany would not hesitate to disturb the peace in order to obtain the hegemony in Europe for herself. The British Government was indeed firmly resolved to oppose any such schemes, and once more King Edward brilliantly served his ministers in setting the diplomatic pace. His endeavours met with success. Spain was won over in 1907; while in Italy, although she still travelled officially in the path of the Triple Alliance, the leaning towards the Western Powers grew more marked from year to year.

After France and England had peacefully settled their differences by the treaty of 1904 and were bound by a close community of interests, the governmental leaders of Italy felt that the interests of their country demanded that they should avoid anything which might displease the statesmen in Paris or contain the germ of possible hostilities with France. Up to this time they had been able to hope that if war broke out between the Dual and the Triple Alliance, England would join forces with Italy, or would at least observe a benevolent neutrality. Now, however, in such a war, they must count upon England's participation as France's ally. They realized that it would be impossible to protect their country against the combined fleets of these two states. The more imminent grew the danger of an Anglo-German war and consequently of a European conflagration, the more irksome the Italian statesmen found their obligations. In addition to this, public opinion in Italy expressed itself more clearly from year to year against the continuance of friendly relations with Austria-Hungary. The cry for an extension of Italy's sphere of influence along the other shore of the Adriatic grew in insistence after the miscarriage of her colonial plans. As the conviction became firmer that these aspirations must be fulfilled against Austria-Hungary's will and not with her help, the voices demanding the abandonment of the existing policy and an open union with the Western Great Powers grew more numerous. If, notwithstanding all this, the Triple Alliance, which expired in July, 1907, was tacitly renewed, it was because Italian statesmen did not consider that the time had come to desert their allies; while Italy's allies, although placing no great trust in Italy's loyalty to the alliance, wished to avoid a break with her that would result in her joining the ranks of her enemies, knowing as they did that such a break would endanger the moral influence of the Central European Alliance.

What, however, was decisive for the further development of the course of events was neither the attitude of Spain nor that of Italy, but the policy of Russia. As we have already seen, German policy was inspired throughout the decade 1895–1905 by the belief that it was always within its power to effect an alliance with Russia. Even after the failure of William II's endeavours to win over the Tsar to an alliance directed against England, he and Bülow clung to the hope that the antagonism between the Russian bear and the British lion would sooner or later result in their coming to grips. But they were doomed to disappointment. They underestimated the change that had taken place in British policy since the close of the Russo-Japanese war. The heavy defeat sustained by Russia had suited British interests, because this defeat prevented Russia from pursuing an active policy detrimental to England in the Far East. England's old and sagacious principle to work for the weakening, but not the complete ruin of her most dangerous Continental enemies, and then to propose reconciliation to them, now caused her to alter her policy in regard to Russia. It is to-day possible to follow from the British documents step by step the whole course of the

negotiations that led first to a *rapprochement* between the
former opponents and finally to the conclusion of an agreement by which the 'arch-enemy' was transformed into a
member of the *Entente*. It is especially interesting to
note that in this case, as in that of France and Germany,
the initiative came from Russia. From the British documents one learns that at the end of 1903, on the eve of the
Russo-Japanese war, conversations had taken place between Benckendorff, the Russian Ambassador at London,
and Lansdowne for the purpose of settling the various
matters at issue between the two Powers in China, Tibet,
and Persia. The outbreak of the war between Russia and
Japan prevented their continuance. The policy pursued
by England during the war contributed only to embitter
these differences between the two countries. The decisive
change came when, on the defeat of Russia, England urged
her ally Japan, that Russia should be granted reasonable
terms of peace; and in point of fact it was not a little due
to England's intervention—though she used her influence
more behind the scenes than openly—that reasonable terms
were granted to Russia in the peace of Portsmouth, in
August, 1905. In so doing England took the first step
towards a lasting understanding with Russia. That the
latter now abandoned her plans of Asiatic conquest and
turned again to seek a way to the open sea through the
Balkans was entirely in accord with England's interests and
removed the principal cause of Anglo-Russian rivalry. England's diplomatic *coup* was first noticeable at the Algeciras
Conference, when Russia sided with Germany's adversaries;
then, more clearly, when Russia's revived endeavours to expand towards south-eastern Europe resulted in a widening
rift in her relations with Turkey and Austria-Hungary.
England gave Russia to understand that Constantinople,
once the apple of discord between them, had no longer
any special interest for her. England's diplomacy succeeded, and this was, perhaps, of particular value in pre-

paring the way for an enduring agreement with Russia. The second Anglo-Japanese treaty of 1905 included the stipulation that neither ally should conclude with a third power a treaty which might prove prejudicial to the other ally. This stipulation presented an insurmountable obstacle in the way of the proposed Anglo-Russian agreement, as long as an amicable understanding was lacking between Russia and Japan. It was to England's interest to bring about this understanding, and she was helped in her endeavour by the controversy which then arose between the United States and Japan over the increasing settlement of Japanese and Chinese labourers in the west of the United States. This Russo-Japanese agreement was finally brought about through the instrumentality of British diplomacy in July, 1907. Soon afterwards, through England's mediation, France concluded with Japan a guarantee treaty concerning China. 'Japan was now allied with England and brought into accord with Russia and France; France allied with Russia, and through the *Entente Cordiale* with England. The quadruple alliance, which was effected during the World War, Russia, France, England, Japan, was thus foreshadowed.' The one thing lacking was an Anglo-Russian *Entente*, and this was soon to come about. The first and most difficult task was the overcoming of Nicholas II's opposition to Russia's separation from Germany. England's attitude in the Russo-Japanese war had not yet been forgotten in St. Petersburg. Count Witte in particular, who for long had been one of the most influential men in the circle surrounding the Tsar, favoured an alliance with Germany and opposed that with England. His resignation in April, 1906, and the appointment as Minister for Foreign Affairs of Isvolski, in place of the dilatory and timid Count Lambsdorf, were distinct assets to England. Isvolski was an admirer of England and a staunch advocate of the view that Russia's reconciliation with England was the necessary hypothesis for the increase of Russia's prestige

in Europe and the world. It has been stated that he desired
then and there to break openly with Germany, but this
statement cannot be substantiated. Isvolski knew that
Nicholas II was not yet prepared for such a course, and
that Russia was far too much weakened by the Japanese
war to hazard a rupture with the Central Powers, even if
she could count upon France's support. He realized that
Russia must be able to count upon England's support
before she could think of breaking with Germany, and
the British and Russian politicians who opened the discussions were agreed upon this point. They could not
hide from themselves the fact that it would be no easy
matter to terminate these discussions successfully, for the
two Powers were still jealous and distrustful of each other
in Persia, Tibet, and Afghanistan.

All these difficulties, however, were comparatively
quickly overcome, not least of all by the conciliatory policy
of England, which was due to Grey's endeavours to remove
the causes of the differences with Russia and to secure the
safety of India against an armed Russian attack or Russian
intrigues. The Treaty signed on August 31, 1907, assigned
to Russia Northern Persia as her sphere of influence. This
entailed a sacrifice on the part of England; but the removal
of the Russian threat to India by the exclusion of Russian
influence from Tibet and Afghanistan was a very important
gain. Thus England had drawn very much nearer her
goal. The old enmity between herself and Russia was
diminished and the way made clear for a still closer
rapprochement. Once again Edward VII used his diplomatic
gifts on England's behalf by convincing the Tsar at their
meeting at Reval in June, 1908, that a closer alliance with
the Western Powers lay nearer to the true interests of
Russia than an alliance with Germany. Hardinge gave
expression to the importance of an Anglo-Russian *entente*
in saying to Isvolski, that in seven or eight years' time a
critical situation might arise in which Russia, if strong in

Europe, might be the arbiter of peace, and have more influence in securing the peace of the world than any Hague Conference. For this reason it would be absolutely necessary for England and Russia to maintain towards each other the same cordial and friendly relations as now existed between England and France.

By the conclusion of the Anglo-Russian treaties one of the most powerful structures known to history was raised. The apparently impossible had come to pass. The former antagonists, France and England, Japan and Russia. Russia and England, were reconciled, and together confronted Germany. Apart from the Franco-Russian alliance, the pillars supporting this structure were the treaties which England concluded in 1902 and 1905 with Japan, the agreements in 1904 with France, and in 1907 and 1908 with Russia. Further supports were formed by the arrangements which made Tripoli over to Italy, and Northern Morocco to Spain. Portugal, England's old vassal, was also included. Russia, for her part, brought more stones to the building by her intrigues in the Balkan States. Serbia, Montenegro, and in some degree Bulgaria, sided with Russia. The system of alliances created by Bismarck had only embraced a great part of the European continent; that of the Triple *Entente* drew within its orbit a great part of the Eastern hemisphere.

If we bring unbiassed judgement to bear upon these events, our verdict will be that the diplomatic brains of the Western Great Powers, particularly of England, were far superior to those of Germany, both in the clearness with which they perceived their goal and in the logical accuracy with which they carried on their negotiations. It must always be considered one of the greatest mistakes made by Germany's leading statesmen, that they maintained in general a passive attitude, in contradistinction to the untiring and ceaseless activity of the French and the British, and that they neglected to follow Bismarck's example in securing allies by satisfying the covetousness of the other Powers. If Bismarck's example had been followed, Germany would have been able to maintain that predominant position which, thanks to his genius and to the activity of her people, she had occupied in the last decades of the nineteenth century.

LECTURE VI

WHEN rumours reached Berlin from St. Petersburg in the autumn of 1906 of an approaching understanding between Russia and England, the Kaiser observed: 'A pretty state of affairs. In future we shall have to deal with the Franco-Russian Alliance, the *Entente Cordiale* between France and England, and the *Entente* between England and Russia; and, in the second place, with Spain, Italy, and Portugal as satellites in this system of alliances.' But Bülow displayed less anxiety, and still held to his opinion that it was impossible for the British lion to lie down in amity with the Russian bear. It was not until after the conclusion of the Anglo-Russian treaty of August 31, 1907, that the governing classes in Berlin seriously began to take account of the danger to Germany arising from an understanding between Russia and England. The Kaiser was advised to express in his meetings with King Edward a desire for an improvement in Anglo-German relations, and Metternich, the German Ambassador at London, was also ordered to give expression to this desire in his conversations with Grey and Haldane. These attempts did not succeed. King Edward and the British Government certainly assured the German Government of their desire to maintain friendly relations with Germany and informed Berlin that nothing was further from their thoughts than to place obstacles in the way of the development of German commerce and colonization, or to harbour plans for an attack upon the German Empire. Time and again, however, they emphasized the fact that, unless Germany reduced her naval armaments, any change in their policy was impossible; for the German naval programme forced England to keep pace in this respect with Germany, imposed great burdens upon the British nation for that purpose, and worked upon public opinion in

England in a sense hostile to Germany. Furthermore, the British Government made it very clear that they were resolved to maintain the existing friendly relations with France and Russia. Germany refused to believe in the peaceful assurances on the part of England. The opinion grew and became more widespread in the German nation that British politicians, especially King Edward, were engaged in an attempt to encircle Germany. The opposition shown by England to an extension of German influence in Asia Minor, the endeavours of the British Government to secure new allies, and, above all, their demands for a reduction in the German naval programme were looked upon as indications of the existence of a feeling of enmity towards Germany. The Press also helped to increase the anti-British feeling. The existence of these beliefs explains the extraordinary excitement aroused in Germany by the news of a meeting between the Tsar and King Edward in Reval. In England this excitement was looked upon as quite unwarranted by the circumstances. Grey told Mensdorff that he utterly failed to comprehend the excitement in Germany. William II—he remarked—had very frequently met the Tsar. Germany had two allies united to her by treaties of alliance. England had only an *Entente* with France, and had only just achieved an agreement with Russia in regard to certain matters in Asia. That was all—nothing more. Secret agreements, alliances, or such-like instruments did not exist; there were absolutely no actions to warrant the belief that England was pursuing a policy of encirclement. Haldane was of the same opinion, and, like Grey, declared that the German naval programme was alone responsible for the anti-German feeling in England. This feeling, Haldane added, would, if things went on as they were going at present, become still stronger in the course of the next five to six years. Metternich reported in the same sense to Berlin, emphasizing King Edward's and the British nation's love of peace, and at the same time stating positively that a concession in the matter of the naval programme was the essential preliminary condition for the establishment of enduring friendly relations between the two Powers.

But he was not listened to, and the exact contrary to what he desired and advised occurred. Bülow declared:

'Agreements which aim at a limitation of our defensive power are not acceptable for discussion by us under any circumstances. A Power which would demand such an agreement from us should be clear in its mind that such a demand would mean war.'

In like manner, but in a more aggressive tone, the Emperor said:

'Count Metternich must be informed that good relations with England at the price of the building of the German Navy are not desired by me. If England intends (graciously) to extend us her hand only with the intimation that we must limit our fleet, this is a pure impertinence, which involves a heavy insult to the German people and their Kaiser, that must be rejected *a limine* by the Ambassador. . . . France and Russia might with equal reason then demand a limitation of our land armaments. The German fleet is not built against any one, and thus not against England, but according to *our* need. That is stated quite clearly in the Naval Bill, and for 11 years has remained unchanged. This law will be carried out to the last iota; whether it suits the British or not does not matter. If they want war, they can begin it; we do not fear it.'

Once more his words showed the direction in which the Kaiser's impetuousness was carrying him. Grey, Haldane, and other British statesmen recognized Germany's right to build her fleet as she desired; they only pointed out that this must of necessity result in a corresponding enlargement of the British fleet and lead to conflicts. Hence they made the proposal that both nations should seek to attain a satisfactory agreement by means of friendly negotiation.

Nevertheless, the Kaiser answered this suggestion, which no one could have possibly regarded as an insult to the German nation or her Kaiser, with a decisive negative. Lloyd George's speech, in which he declared that the British Navy must be stronger than the German in order to afford England a feeling of security and the power to check any designs that Germany might harbour of attacking England, was commented upon as follows by the Kaiser: 'That is a language that up to the present has only been permitted in addressing China or Italy or such fellows.' He replied to the proposal for a slowing-down in the rate of naval construction with the remark: 'No! Three times "No"; after Lloyd George's speech "Never".' The Kaiser declared British fears of a naval attack upon the island by the German fleet to be a figment of the imagination, 'an absurd piece of stupidity'. Nevertheless, his endeavours in his conversations with King Edward, with British naval experts, and in his correspondence with Lord Tweedmouth, to prove that he harboured no designs upon British naval supremacy, failed to carry conviction, since he would not take the one step—agreement to a slowing-down of the rate of naval construction—that would have been successful in removing the fears by which England was animated. With ever increasing firmness the idea held by Tirpitz became fixed in the Emperor's mind: the idea that the risk involved in a continuation of the naval programme was comparable to that incurred by a man forced to live through a definitely limited period of time in which he might encounter danger. Furthermore, Tirpitz believed that, as the German fleet grew in strength so England would become ever more and more hesitant in taking action against Germany. This conviction on the part of the Emperor and Tirpitz rendered fruitless all endeavours at conciliation made by those German statesmen 'who did not believe that this so-called "danger zone" had any definite time limit attached to it, inasmuch as

England was in a position to compete in the race by keeping up the old standard of naval strength as between herself and Germany'; and who further believed that the increase in German naval armaments only served to strengthen anti-German feeling in England and to render impossible the much-desired agreement with that country. Bülow shared the Emperor's views, and incited his Imperial master to hold to them with increasing tenacity.

The sole justification for the Emperor's policy would have been the acquisition by Germany of allies powerful enough to be of assistance to her in the event of an outbreak of war with England. Under the existing international conditions any prospect of gaining such allies had virtually been excluded; nor was such a possibility ever seriously envisaged in Berlin. The German Government relied on its own strength and on that of one of its allies—Austria-Hungary. When the *Entente* between England and Russia became an accomplished fact, Bülow outlined the policy to be followed by Germany in the future as follows:

'Germany and Austria-Hungary form a solid structure that is capable of weathering all storms. The existing alliance, which is founded upon a community of interests and a common reverence for monarchism, is the best security for the two Monarchies against other Powers that are possibly inspired with revolutionary ideals and anti-autocratic feelings. A faithful co-operation with Austria-Hungary must and shall remain in the future the basic principle of German foreign policy.'

The Kaiser placed on the margin of the memorandum containing these words an emphatic 'Yes'.

An opportunity speedily came for testing this policy. In the beginning of October, 1908, Francis Joseph announced to the Great Powers of Europe the annexation of Bosnia and Herzegovina, occupied by Austria-Hungary in the year 1878. Taken in the abstract this was not an event of world importance, since no change took place in respect of territory. But in reality it has been considered, and not without reason, to be one of the most important historical facts in the first decade of the twentieth century, as the new grouping of the Great Powers, England, France, Russia on the one side, Germany, Austria-Hungary, Italy on the other, was then clearly seen for the first time, a grouping which remained unaltered until the beginning of the World War.

Since the foundation of the German Empire and of the kingdom of United Italy, an extension of Austria-Hungary towards the south and west of Europe had been impossible. Only in the south-east could she still count on an expansion of her territory and influence. Thus from the seventies onwards the policy of the leading statesmen of Austria-Hungary had taken the direction indicated by geographical conditions. In this direction she had had to reckon with the opposition of Russia, which, with the pressing back of Turkish influence, had become her great rival in south-eastern Europe. In order to maintain herself as a Great Power, render her frontiers secure against hostile attacks, and suffer no restriction of her further development towards the south-east, Austria-Hungary could not allow another Great Power to command the Danube and its mouths and arrogate to itself the hegemony of the Balkan peoples. And the danger threatening from Russia increased with the growing of the pan-Slavic movement, which found enthusiastic followers among the Slav subjects of the Danube monarchy.

In their endeavours to defend their independence against the Germans and especially against the increasing aggressiveness of the Magyars, the South Slavs cast ever more longing glances across the border at their brethren in Serbia and lent their ear to the enticements of those who represented the idea of a greater Serbia. The danger increased when the Karageorgievic dynasty, protected by Russia, ascended the Serbian throne. From now on, Belgrade became the centre of all Pan-Serbian agitations;

from there was preached incessantly the struggle against the Danube monarchy, whose powerful position in the Balkans was described as the only obstacle to the realization of the nationalist desires of all South Slavs. Russia was appealed to by Belgrade as a friend in need, and her leading statesmen became increasingly inclined to answer the call. Thus the danger of a conflict between Austria and Russia increased from year to year and was intensified after the Russo-Japanese war. For, as a consequence of the latter, the Russian statesmen now abandoned the policy of reaching the warm seas in the Far East and returned to that of Peter and Catherine, never entirely given up, the goal of which was the conquest of Constantinople, the command of the Dardanelles, and the hegemony in the Balkan Peninsula. Austria soon recognized the danger from this side to her position as a Great Power, which now became ever more menacing in the measure in which the internal affairs of the Turkish Empire assumed a more critical aspect.

Aehrenthal, who since 1906 had been in control of Austria-Hungary's foreign policy, was, in agreement with the German statesmen, desirous of preserving Turkey; at the same time, however, he was firmly determined to safeguard the interests of the Dual Monarchy. For this reason, when the revolution of the Young Turks in July, 1908, gave cause to fear a change of Turkish foreign policy unfavourable to Austria-Hungary, he decided on a bold *coup*. It seemed probable that the new Turkish Government would invite the inhabitants of Bosnia and Herzegovina to send representatives to the Turkish Parliament, and also that the Turkish Parliament would come out strongly for Turkey's rights over these provinces, rights which formally still existed. Aehrenthal was firmly of the opinion that it was therefore necessary to make sure of the possession of these provinces, which had for the past thirty years been under Austro-Hungarian government, and for which the monarchy had done so much in improving their commercial and cultural conditions. It happened opportunely that at this very time, Isvolski, who then directed Russian foreign policy, wished definitely to realize Russian aims regarding the Dardanelles. Negotiations were opened, and on the 15th of September, 1908, a verbal agreement was arrived at. Isvolski gave his consent to the annexation of Bosnia and Herzegovina in the event of the Viennese Government falling in with his plans regarding the Straits.

It is not possible here to dwell upon the question as to who of the two statesmen was attempting to outwit the other; or whether they had both intended to keep open to themselves a door of escape. Certain it is, however, that neither expected serious opposition on the part of the Western Powers in the pursuit of their plans. When, however, at the beginning of October, 1908, Francis Joseph publicly announced the annexation of Bosnia and Herzegovina as a *fait accompli*, a storm of indignation burst forth in many quarters.

It is not part of my subject to treat of the intricate diplomatic struggles which were a consequence of Aehrenthal's policy. After several months of exciting negotiations, which several times threatened to come to grief, and after it had looked for a while as if a decision must be obtained by force of arms, Isvolski found himself compelled to beat a retreat; for Germany resolutely took her stand by the side of the Habsburg monarchy, while France, her gaze riveted upon her Moroccan interests, gave but lukewarm support to the demands of her Russian ally. Thus Russia, who had not yet recovered from the defeat she had suffered in the Russo-Japanese war, dared not draw the sword.

What policy had been followed by England during these critical months? The publication of the British diplomatic documents enables us to follow British policy at the time of the Balkan crisis step by step. They reveal that the view entertained by the ruling circles of Austria-Hungary and

Germany that British statesmen, Grey above all others, were working to stir up Turkey and Serbia to aggressive action against the Danubian monarchy had no substantiation in fact. At the same time they reveal that England strongly disapproved of Aehrenthal's action. The reply of King Edward to the letter in which Francis Joseph announced to him the annexation plainly reveals this; it is still more clearly shown in Grey's observations to Mensdorff. Grey emphasized most forcibly that Aehrenthal's action was in contradiction with international agreements, of which the Berlin Treaty was one, which could only be altered by the consent of all the signatory Powers. When Mensdorff sought to justify Aehrenthal's action by remarking that he was forced to act as he had done, because of the constitutional issue, and that he could not have first asked for Turkey's assent, seeing that, in event of her refusal, he would still have had to annex Bosnia and Herzegovina, Grey replied as follows: 'That amounts to this: One partner has done something without consulting the other partner about it, because he knew that the other partner would object to it; then, having done it, the first partner turned to the other and said: "Please do not mind after all".' Grey accused Aehrenthal of pursuing an aggressive policy and of disturbing the peace. 'I cannot believe in Aehrenthal's word of honour statement,' wrote King Edward, 'as facts belie it.'

Aehrenthal, on the other hand, accused the British politicians of seeking to counteract Austria's proper interests everywhere—as formerly in Macedonia and the Sanjak railway affair, so now in disputes with Serbia, with Russia, and with Turkey. Aehrenthal's accusations, in as far as they applied to Grey, were not wholly justified. But a study of the British documents reveals that Grey, although not inspired by any sympathy for the enemies of the Danubian monarchy, was nevertheless anxious to fulfil their wishes, and especially those of Russia, in as far as it was possible to do so while safeguarding the maintenance of peace and the special interests of England. For it was of the greatest advantage to England that Russia should no longer employ her full strength in the Far East, and that she should instead devote her attention to the Balkan Peninsula.

It was not at all in accordance with Grey's own wishes that the Balkan crisis ended with the retreat of Russia brought about by German influence; and the stormy debates in Vienna between Cartwright and Aehrenthal over the conditions for a settlement between Serbia and the Danubian monarchy show how wide the gulf had become which separated the two Governments. The Annexation crisis resulted in a triumph for the Central Empires, but it was a Pyrrhic victory, because through it the cleavage of Europe into two hostile camps became more obvious than ever. While the German 'Nibelungentreue' had successfully proved its worth, it had resulted in Russia's decision to break definitely with Austria-Hungary and had increased her hostility to German policy. At that time Isvolski said to Sir Arthur Nicolson, the British Ambassador at St. Petersburg, that it had been exceedingly painful for him to have to give way, but 'the Austro-German combination was stronger than the Triple *Entente*'. On Nicolson's seeking to deny this, the Russian replied that 'this might be so in a sense; but there is no alliance binding the three Powers together and there is not that firmness and cohesion that existed between Austria and Germany'. With this conversation fresh in mind, Nicolson wrote on March 24 to Grey:

'My firm opinion is, that both Germany and Austria are carrying out a line of policy and action carefully prepared and thought out. Algeciras had to be revenged, the "Ring" broken through and the Triple *Entente* dissipated. The Franco-German agreement [this reference is to the Agreement of February, 1909, over Morocco] was the first step and France

is a quarter of the way towards a fuller understanding with
Germany. Russia is temporarily weak with a timorous Foreign
Minister. She has to be frightened out of the *Entente* and the
first step towards this has been eminently successful. The
Franco-Russian alliance has not borne the test and the Anglo-
Russian *Entente* is not sufficiently strong or sufficiently deep-
rooted to have any appreciable influence. The hegemony of
the Central Powers will be established in Europe, and England
will be isolated. . . . When we have passed through the present
"Sturm und Drang" period, I should not be surprised if we were
to find both France and Russia gravitating towards the Central
Powers, as neither of the former, distrustful of each other, feels
that she can stand alone against the power of the central
combination. Our *Entente*, I much fear, will languish and
possibly die. If it were possible to extend and strengthen it by
bringing it nearer to the nature of an alliance, it would then be
possible to deter Russia from moving towards Berlin. . . . The
ultimate aims of Germany surely are, without doubt, to obtain
the preponderance on the continent of Europe; and when she
is strong enough, and apparently she is making very strenuous
efforts to become so, she will enter on a contest with us for
maritime supremacy. In past time we have had to fight
Holland, Spain, and France for this supremacy, and, personally,
I am convinced that, sooner or later, we shall have to repeat
the same struggle with Germany.'

Now it is very characteristic of Grey's whole policy that he
was decisively opposed to such far-reaching schemes.

'I do not think', he wrote to Nicolson on April 2, 1909, 'that
it is practicable to change our agreements into alliances; the
feeling here about definite commitment to a continental war
on unforseeable conditions would be too dubious to permit
us to make an alliance. Russia, too, must make her internal
government less reactionary; till she does, liberal sentiment
will remain very cool, and even those who are not sentimental
will not believe that Russia can purge her administration
sufficiently to become a strong and reliable power. Meanwhile,
let us keep an *entente* with Russia in the sense of keeping in

touch, so that our diplomatic action with Russia may be in accord and in mutual support.'

In these words Grey clearly foreshadowed the policy he pursued in the following years—a policy of strengthening the *Entente* while avoiding any binding obligations that could restrict England's liberty of action in the future. Towards Germany his policy displayed a willingness to promote better relations, while at the same time he avoided taking any step which could have given his *Entente* friends cause for complaint or suspicion. As the essential pre-liminary condition for an understanding with Germany, he demanded a more conciliatory policy on her part in the naval question. 'Europe', he said at that time, 'is divided into two camps, and it will be very difficult to bring all the Powers within one camp. Nevertheless, friendly rela-tions with Germany are possible, if she is willing to meet England's wishes in the naval question.' When the resigna-tion of Bülow, and the appointment of Bethmann-Hollweg as his successor, opened up the prospect of a possibly successful resumption of the negotiations that had never been allowed entirely to drop, Grey still remained true to these basic principles in his policy. Both sides were in earnest in resuming the negotiations. Bethmann-Hollweg did all in his power to reach an understanding with England—an understanding which he looked upon as the essential condition for the future prosperity of Germany. He was all in favour of meeting England in the naval question without putting forward conditions which England could only fulfil by coming into conflict with her allies. He did not ask for any general political understanding, or any neutrality treaty; he was prepared to be satisfied with a declaration on the part of the British Government that they were ready to adopt a friendly policy towards Germany and that the *Entente* was not aimed at Germany. Beth-mann was successful in winning over both the Emperor and Tirpitz to this policy, at least in principle. Grey hailed this conciliatory attitude with joy. Nevertheless, the negotiations had scarcely begun when it became apparent that the differences were too great to be surmounted. The Kaiser and Tirpitz were still unwilling to make concessions of any importance in the naval question, while Grey refused to conclude a political agreement in the sense desired by the Kaiser. In a letter to Goschen dated September 1, 1909, Grey defined his standpoint with great clarity.

'There is nothing in our agreements with France and Russia', he wrote, 'which is directed against Germany and therefore nothing to bar a friendly arrangement with Germany. But we have no general political understanding formulated either with Russia or France; and to do with Germany what has not been done with Russia and France would look as if we are intending to change friends. I want a good understanding with Germany; but it must be one which will not imperil those which we have with France and Russia. I should have thought some formula could be found to which they (France and Russia) might also be parties; that would be the best and most reassuring solution; though I see that the French could not be a party to anything that looked like confirming the loss of Alsace-Lorraine.'

The importance of this latter sentence must be immediately apparent to every critical reader. Grey was convinced that France would not give up the idea of revenge, and therefore he did not wish to undertake any obligation which might be construed into a recognition of the Peace of Frankfort and of the permanent incorporation of Alsace-Lorraine in the German Empire. Thus it becomes easier to understand why the Anglo-German negotiations, which were often broken off and as often resumed during the years 1909–10, led to no result other than that both sides blamed each other for their failure, and that public opinion in both countries became increasingly inflamed. In the autumn of 1910, when the Persian question brought about a difference of opinion between the Russian and

British Governments, and Russia and Germany seemed
for a moment to come into closer relations, Bethmann
initiated fresh negotiations with England with the object
of achieving a political and naval agreement. Once
more these negotiations broke down because Germany
demanded the conclusion of a political agreement as an
indispensable preliminary to any concessions on her part
in the naval question. The failure of these negotiations was
followed by a storm of protest in Germany against British
policy in Morocco and Persia, which ran counter to German
commercial interests in those countries, and against the
suspicion with which every action of the German Government was regarded in London. These protests were rejected by the Foreign Office as unfounded, but they only
served to widen the gulf between the two countries still
further. The visit of the Tsar to the Kaiser in Potsdam in
November, 1910, gave rise to furious attacks in the British
Press on the Kaiser and his advisers. Russia—it was said
—was on the way to being separated from her friends; the
Kaiser and Tirpitz were planning an attack upon the
British fleet. The distrust of Germany grew still greater
in governmental circles in England. While it is true that
nobody believed Bethmann to be inspired with hostile
intentions towards England, it was believed that he was
not strong enough to defend his policy against the attacks
made upon it by the Emperor, Tirpitz, the German Navy
League, and the great industrialists. When, in the spring
of 1911, the German Government replied to a renewed
inquiry from the British Government, as to whether an
agreement in the naval question was still possible, with the
declaration that the time for a reduction of the German
naval programme was past, and at the same time once
again demanded the conclusion of the political agreement
so often refused by England, the opponents of Germany in
England found fresh fuel added to their fires. Nevertheless, Grey was resolved to carry on the negotiations with

Germany, and they were still in progress when the Moroccan question provoked fresh conflicts between Germany and France. England found herself involved in disputes that led to such a cleavage between the Western Powers and Germany that for a long time the outbreak of war appeared imminent. Since the conclusion of the treaty of February, 1909, France had aimed at bringing Morocco completely within her power, and in 1911 an expedition was fitted out for the purpose of occupying Fez. The German public grew more and more excited from month to month, and demanded energetic action by the Government even more insistently than they had done in 1905 and 1909. Kiderlen-Wächter, who at that moment was the real inspirer of German foreign policy, did not hesitate to head public opinion, and he convinced the Imperial Chancellor and the Emperor that an active policy would lead to Germany's receiving valuable compensations from France in return for the abandonment of German rights in Morocco. On July 1, the small German cruiser *Panther* appeared in Agadir for the purpose of backing up this policy. A storm of indignation in Paris and London followed her appearance. In London it was thought that Germany intended to settle permanently in Southern Morocco—a course which was felt to be inimical to British interests. Grey demanded an explanation of Germany's plans in Africa, and demanded also that England should be admitted to the negotiations that had hitherto been carried on between France and Germany alone. On the same day Lloyd George delivered a speech in which he said:

'If a situation were to be forced upon us in which peace could only be preserved by the surrender of the great and beneficent position Britain had won . . . by allowing Britain to be treated, where her interests were vitally affected, as if she were of no account in the Cabinet of nations, then I say emphatically that peace at that price would be a humiliation for a great country like ours to endure.'

This warning to Germany was looked upon in Berlin as a threat to which it was not possible to give way. When, however, Metternich, by order of Kiderlen, informed Grey that Germany had no intention of permanently settling in Morocco, or of creating a naval base at Agadir, the clouds once more rolled away.

The sole object of German policy—Metternich declared —was to induce France to come either to a friendly arrangement with Germany by means of concessions in the Congo, or else to return to the arrangement contained in the Algeciras Agreement. Grey declared that he felt 'relieved' by this declaration, and he added that nothing was further from his intention than to put obstacles in the way of an understanding between France and Germany. England had no objection to German colonial expansion in Central Africa. Nevertheless, under the impression created by Lloyd George's speech, it was believed in Germany that England was making all preparations for a war with Germany; an opinion that was only strengthened by a statement of a British Member of Parliament, Captain Faber, in November, 1911, which was misunderstood and falsely reported in Berlin, to the effect that in the previous summer England was on the verge of war. To-day it can with confidence be said that at that time there was no desire in England for a war with Germany, and furthermore that England had not endeavoured to stir up the French to war. What is certain is that the British Government was determined to support France in the event of a war with Germany: a resolve that was not denied nor concealed by Grey. But the danger of war passed away. In November, 1911, after long and wearisome negotiations, an agreement was reached between France and Germany. Germany abandoned her rights in Morocco in return for an extension of the Cameroons at the cost of the French Congo: a poor return in comparison with the bitterness which had been aroused in France and England by

Germany's action, a bitterness that helped to cement the *Entente* and to strengthen the conviction widely held in France that she would be able to count upon British support in the event of the outbreak of a Franco-German war.

The danger by which Germany had been seriously threatened in the summer of 1911, of having to face not only France and Russia, but England as well, had a great yet dissimilar effect upon the Kaiser and Tirpitz on the one side and on Bethmann on the other. The Kaiser and Tirpitz came to the conclusion that the work on the construction of the German fleet must be continued even more vigorously in order that it might be ready for all emergencies. In vain did Metternich warn the Kaiser against too great haste. He declared that in many influential political circles in England it was said that it would have been dreadful if England—as was nearly the case in 1909 and 1911—had been involved in war not for any real and vital interest of her own, but for the sake of Russian influence in the Balkans, or French supremacy in Morocco. Moreover, he reported Grey as being animated by a sincere desire to promote better relations with Germany. Yet at the same time he did not fail to state that Grey made it clear that England would have nothing to do with a political agreement which involved a renunciation of the *Entente*; but that he was willing to give Germany support in developing a colonial empire in Central Africa. As a preliminary, however, both Grey and Haldane demanded concessions from Germany in the naval question, and, as he had done in the past, so now Metternich advised that British wishes should be fulfilled in this respect as far as possible. He further voiced his conviction that if Germany were again to increase her fleet, and thereby compel England to similar measures and fresh expenditure, any reconciliation would become impossible; and the *Entente* would probably harden into an actual alliance. The

Kaiser, however, was annoyed by Metternich's remarks. 'Had I followed him,' he said, 'then we should have no fleet at all by now. His deduction tolerates the interference of a foreign nation in our naval policy, that, as Supreme War Lord and Kaiser, I neither shall nor can allow. And what a humiliation for our people! The supplementary bill must be carried out. The poor fellow' [Metternich] 'is beyond help. We are not to arm and England will stay good-humoured. That is all.' Hence he agreed to Tirpitz's plans, and pushed them on regardless of the consequences. Tirpitz had drafted a new Navy Bill to be introduced in 1912, which would result in an important augmentation of the German fleet, and he was busy preparing public opinion so as to render easy the acceptance of this Bill by the Reichstag. Bethmann-Hollweg did not share his sovereign's views, and was determined to embark upon a different course. He has clearly indicated in his *Reflections on the World War* the aims towards which his policy at this date was directed. 'I wished', he said, 'to draw the poison-fangs of the Russo-French alliance by an understanding with England.' He felt that Germany was no longer strong enough to keep two irons in the fire. London was rightly considered by him to be the centre of the Triple *Entente*. If Germany were on friendly terms with England, the danger threatening from east and west could be averted. A direct exchange of views seemed to him desirable, and negotiations were indeed initiated through the intermediary of Ernest Cassel and Ballin. The British proposals, which were approved by Churchill, Grey, and Lloyd George, were based on the principle 'that England's superiority at sea must be maintained, the German naval programme must not be increased, but diminished wherever possible; that England is prepared to support Germany's colonial expansion as far as possible, and to entertain proposals for an agreement which excludes its participation in all *aggressive* plans or combinations against Germany'. Bethmann was quite ready to meet British demands, but was forced, under pressure from his colleagues, to lay down the condition 'that the proposed estimates for 1912 were ranked as part of the existing naval programme'; a demand which Metternich at once declared could never be accepted by England. Metternich advised Bethmann to insist that the word 'aggressive' should be struck out of the draft of the proposed political agreement. Any such agreement would be worthless so long as the word 'aggressive' remained, since the aims of the *Entente* and the attitude of England in 1909 and 1911 were not regarded by England as aggressive. Mention is made of these differences here, since it was because of them that the negotiations, opened in the spring of 1912, finally broke down. The British Cabinet resolved to send Haldane to Berlin, though not with authority to conclude a binding agreement, as was believed in Germany. His main task was to find out if there really was a sincere desire in Berlin for friendly negotiations; that is to say, a willingness to renounce the proposed Naval Bill. Bethmann received him sympathetically, but he met with a cooler reception from Tirpitz and the Emperor. Under such circumstances Haldane's mission failed to fulfil either the hopes of the Germans or the expectations of the English. Germany held that the most important thing was the conclusion of a political agreement; Bethmann wanted a promise of benevolent neutrality and of help in localizing the conflict so far as possible, in the event of one of the powers being involved in war with one or more opponents. Haldane declared that England could not go further than to promise that neither of the contracting powers should make an unprovoked attack upon the other, nor join any coalition which intended to attack the other, nor take part in plans and undertakings with these aims in view. But Germany would not be satisfied with this: she demanded unqualified neutrality. A like fate attended the negotiations between the two countries in colonial matters. The decisive event, however, in all these negotiations was the failure of Bethmann-Hollweg to induce Tirpitz and the Kaiser to make real concessions to England in the naval issue. The most he could achieve was that Haldane was given a copy of the proposed Naval Bill for the purpose of information and future use in discussions, and also the promise that its execution should be postponed for a year in the event of an understanding being reached in the question of the political agreement. Nevertheless, all further attempts to achieve a settlement of this question proved unavailing. The British Government refused to accept a clause which Metternich proposed to them, and which ran as follows: 'England will therefore naturally maintain a benevolent neutrality should Germany be forced into war.' Under the influence of Russia and France, who had watched the negotiations between Germany and England with distrust and anxiety, Grey declared: 'As Germany is again strengthening her navy, England could not imperil her old friendship. A direct neutrality agreement would inevitably offend French susceptibilities.' The German Government replied to this statement by laying the naval supplementary bill before the Reichstag, and it became law on May 14. This was the step which marked the turn in the march of events. In England people were now convinced that it was not possible to compass a reduction of naval armaments in Germany by means of an agreement. It must be pointed out also that it was a further step on the road which led to the World War, for England set about strengthening the Triple *Entente* with greater energy than before. In the spring of 1912, England promised military assistance to Belgium in the event of an invasion of Belgium by German troops. At the same time, relations between England and Russia improved, as a result of the compromise reached in the Persian question. In July, another important step was

taken in the strengthening of the Triple *Entente*. A
Franco-Russian naval treaty, supplementing the military
treaty of 1892, was concluded in Paris, which aimed at the
linking up of the French and Russian fleets in the event of
a war against Germany. Then Poincaré, since January,
1912, the head of the French Cabinet, entered into further
important agreements. Russia undertook, with the aid of
French capital, to extend her railway system westwards.
Poincaré promised to increase the term of compulsory military service to three years. An Anglo-French naval agreement followed, by which the two states undertook recipro-
cally to entrust to each other the protection of their
interests. England strengthened her home fleet by trans-
ferring to it a part of her Mediterranean fleet, and in
return France removed practically all of her squadron to
her south coast, so that she now took a share in the protection of England's Mediterranean interests. England
undertook to protect the French coast on the English
channel and the Atlantic. The conclusion of these naval
and military agreements rendered the French politicians all
the more conscious of the lack of a written political treaty,
and they believed that the time had now come to make
good this deficiency. By the desire of Poincaré, Cambon,
the French Ambassador at London, addressed a formal
request to Grey for a written agreement. This agreement
should determine in what circumstances either Power
could count upon armed assistance from the other. The
British Government, particularly Grey, took up the
suggestion only with great caution. Grey did not wish
to leave the decision as to war or peace to the discretion of
the excitable French temperament, but rather to reserve
to England freedom of action. He had also to consider the
British Parliament, in which a majority would not hear of
an actual war treaty. He insisted that a treaty must be
known and approved by the whole Cabinet, and that he
could therefore not agree to a formal diplomatic document.

Instead, only letters were exchanged between Grey and
Cambon. And in his letter of November 22, 1912, Grey
stressed the fact that while 'from time to time in recent years
the French and British naval and military experts have consulted together, it has always been understood that such
consultation does not restrict the freedom of either Government to decide at any further time whether or not to assist
the other by armed force'. He then went on to declare, in
the sense desired by Cambon: 'I agree that, if either Government had grave reason to expect an unprovoked attack by
a third Power, or something that threatened the general
peace, it should immediately discuss with the other
whether both Governments should act together to prevent
aggression and to preserve peace, and, if so, what measures
they would be prepared to take in common.' Observe
with what caution the agreements were arrived at by
England. The British nation was not bound by the
agreement; only the Government then in power. Furthermore, England reserved to herself the right of deciding
whether or not she would take part in a Franco-German
war; she could do so, but she was not under obligation to
do so. She bound herself neither in a political nor in a
military sense. Nevertheless, it was certainly a moral
engagement in which Grey involved his country, an
engagement that assured to French statesmen the hope
that in a war with Germany France would be supported
not only by the Russian, but also by the British army and
navy. It is possible that Grey in making this agreement
with France was also pursuing another object: that of
assuring to England the right to intervene in a mediatory
sense in the event of the outbreak of a Franco-German
war or of an Austro-Russian conflict in which France and
Germany might also be involved. For at the very time that
Grey and Cambon completed the exchange of notes the
long-threatened war between the Christian states of the
Balkans and Turkey had broken out—a war that might

have been extended by the intervention of Austria-Hungary and Russia, and that even gave rise to fears lest it might be the signal for a European conflagration. That this danger was averted was due in the first place to the mediatory role filled by Grey and the British Government: it was also due to them that the Balkan States, who had been made arrogant by victory, were kept under control. At the Conference of Ambassadors, which met in London under Grey's presidency from December, 1912, onward, a compromise was achieved between Austria-Hungary and Russia, which, indeed, did not wholly satisfy either Power, but which was at least successful in preventing the outbreak of the war between them that had on several occasions seemed unavoidable. Germany was also active in the same sense as England. England used her influence with Russia; Germany used hers with Austria-Hungary. While Grey told the Russian Government that public opinion would not tolerate Europe being the scene of a world war for the sake of some Balkan issue, the German Government told its Austrian ally that it was not prepared to throw the existence of Germany into the scale in order to enable Austria to pursue her attempts to extend her sphere of influence in the Balkans. On the renewal of the Triple Alliance in December, 1912, the Chancellor declared that it is intended to serve the cause of European peace, and not a craving for conquest on the part of its members; that it is intended to be an insurance, not an aggressive co-operative society. It would become necessary for Germany to leave her allies to face alone the danger which an attempt to add to their possessions would evoke. Only if her allies were to be victims of unprovoked attacks, or if it were necessary to defend her own standing in Europe, her future, or her security, would Germany call her soldiers to arms. And the Kaiser wrote to Bethmann-Hollweg: 'The alliance with Austria-Hungary compels us to march in the event of her being attacked by Russia. Then France will be dragged in and England will not remain quiet. . . . It is not the intention of the Treaty of Alliance that we should be compelled to embark on a war of life and death at the caprice of our allies, without there being any threat to a vital interest of those allies.'

The co-operation between British and German diplomatists in the London Conference awoke once more the desire in both Governments to effect a settlement of the existing differences. The British Government expressed its full confidence in Bethmann-Hollweg, and King George told Mensdorff in March, 1913, that he was always willing to come to an understanding with Germany. The Imperial Chancellor spoke on April 8, 1913, in the Reichstag, in the warmest terms of the part played by Grey in the London Conference, and he laid emphasis on the fact that he thought co-operation between Germany and England to be the best thing for the peace of Europe. But he knew that this was impossible without an agreement on the naval issue. Hence he once more endeavoured to win over the Kaiser and Tirpitz to make concessions, but once more he met with a definite refusal. They were only prepared to make concessions of any value, if England was also ready to give binding pledges that she would remain neutral in the event of a Continental war. Out of regard for the *Entente*, and the obligations he had undertaken towards his allies, Grey could not and would not give any such pledges. Thus it came about that he, and many of his colleagues in the Cabinet, continued to believe in the aggressive designs of Germany. Grey said to Mensdorff: 'The Germans know all our charts, the best landing-places, the roads on the coast. England, on the other hand, could not land troops in Germany, for they would be immediately wiped out; but the same could not be said with truth of German troops landing in England.' And Churchill said: 'The great naval armaments of Germany brought those of England into existence. If any one points a pistol at me, beautiful speeches are of no use. I must defend myself against the threat. Cold and formal relations between Berlin and London are all that one can hope for.' Nor was Haldane much more optimistic. He rejoiced—so he told Mensdorff —at the improvement in Anglo-German relations; he hoped that some lasting good would remain. At the same time he emphasized the fact that there could be no question of a change in alliances or '*ententes*'. Yet better relations between individual members of the two different groups might benefit the relationship of groups. Bethmann-Hollweg seized upon the suggestion. He hoped that through agreements in individual questions the ground might be prepared for the conclusion of a general understanding with England; and Grey displayed his willingness to meet him half way. Negotiations were initiated for the purpose of achieving agreement in the Portuguese colonies question and in that of the Baghdad railway. As they led to a successful result, hope awoke that day by day agreements would be attained in other issues; and that in the end a general understanding would come to life. No sooner had this hope been born than signs arose to indicate that a permanent understanding between the two Powers was rendered impossible by their contending and contrary interests and their obligations in opposing directions.

The outcome of the Balkan wars meant for the Central Powers, especially for Austria-Hungary, a notable loss of prestige in the Balkan Peninsula. Intoxicated by their success against the Turks, the Serbs more and more openly displayed their enmity towards the Danubian monarchy. Their demands were supported by the Russian Government. The anti-Austrian party in Rumania became more and more active. The danger of a new Balkan league under Russian leadership grew from month to month. The German Government invariably sought to use their influence in Vienna in a pacific sense, yet they could not close their eyes to the fact that the danger of a war between

Russia and their ally grew daily more imminent. The violent opposition aroused in Russia by the German Emperor's endeavour to effect a re-organization of the Turkish army by German officers helped to increase the ill-feeling that had arisen between Berlin and St. Petersburg.

The apparent growth of friendship between England and Germany had caused anxiety in Paris and St. Petersburg. In order to be prepared for a war against the Central Powers France introduced the three-year term of compulsory military service. Russia increased her army and built strategical railways to facilitate the transport of large bodies of troops to the German and Austrian frontiers. Since, however, both Germany and Austria also added to their military strength at the same time, French and Russian statesmen could only reckon on a victory if they were assured that England would fight on their side. Hence they urged the British Government to change the *entente* into an alliance. Grey persistently rejected all such proposals. He assured them that no change had taken place in his policy and that no change would take place. In the spring of 1914, although unwillingly, he gave his assent to the pressing demands of his allies for the initiation of negotiations that should lead to an Anglo-Russian naval agreement. As the negotiations with Germany over the Portuguese colonies and the Baghdad railway had then come to a successful conclusion, he let it be understood that, although willing to abide by the obligations he had undertaken in regard to his allies, he did not wish to close the path to better relations with Germany.

The rumours of an approaching Anglo-Russian naval agreement aroused great excitement in the German press, although German statesmen attached little importance to them and were fully satisfied with Grey's denial in the House of Commons that any secret treaties existed which restrained England's liberty of action in the event of an outbreak of war. He added that no negotiations had ever taken place having for their object the conclusion of any such treaties. This declaration, which was followed by a similar one on the part of Asquith, as well as the successful issue of the Anglo-German negotiations for an agreement on reciprocal interests in Africa and Asia, strengthened the conviction of German and Austro-Hungarian statesmen that no danger was to be expected from England; and that, in event of the outbreak of a European war, England would not take any active part in it. When Lichnowsky in February, 1914, as on many previous occasions, declared that England would certainly take the side of the enemies of the Central Powers, Jagow, the German Secretary of State, replied: 'I must confess I think that you are often too pessimistic: especially when you declare that in any eventuality England will be found at the side of France in the event of a war. We have not built our fleet for nothing, and in my opinion England will think very carefully over the question whether it is so easy and so harmless to play the part of guardian angel to France.' The Central Powers, therefore, thought that they could devote their whole attention to the Near East, where conditions pressed for a decision, since it was believed that Russia was at work to renew the Balkan league, that Turkey would be included in it, and that such a combination would threaten the existence of the Dual Monarchy. In a memorandum intended for the German Government, Berchtold, the Austro-Hungarian Minister for Foreign Affairs, emphasized the urgency of making every effort to anticipate the Russians and to form a Balkan league under the leadership of the Central Powers, which should include Bulgaria, Roumania, Greece, and Turkey, and have for its objective the suppression of Serbia as a political power in the Balkans. Before this document was dispatched to Berlin, the news arrived in Vienna that Francis Ferdinand, the heir to the crown of Austria-Hungary, and his consort, had been murdered at Sarajevo, the capital of Bosnia, by Austrian subjects of Serb nationality. With his tragic end a new period began, not only in the history of Austria-Hungary but in that of the world; a period which led to the most bloody war mankind has ever seen.

With this I draw to a close. You will have noticed that I have refrained in these lectures from dealing with the causes of the World War and from discussing the question of what degree of so-called guilt—I should prefer to say responsibility—rests on individual people, not to say individual men, for having precipitated it. I have done so because it is my firm conviction that these causes are too manifold and deep-rooted to be summed up in the common phrases about Austria-Hungary's wishes to expand her sphere of influence in the Balkans, Germany's striving for world-standing and world-power, Russia's longing for the open sea, the irresistible desire of France to recover Alsace-Lorraine, or England's uneasiness about the growth of Germany's fleet. To inquire more deeply into the nature of the real causes of the World War would necessitate a detailed account, not only of the foreign policy, but also of the internal development of all the European Powers; an inquiry into the predominance of the idea of nationality throughout Europe during the nineteenth and twentieth centuries; investigations into the rivalry of the European states in commerce and in the acquisition of colonies as outlets for their rapidly increasing population and as markets for their goods and industrial products. It would necessitate researches into the nature of the struggle, especially in the three Eastern Great Powers, for self-government; into the reaction upon the international situation of the exaggerated military and naval armaments; into the atmosphere of mutual suspicion that gradually grew up; and last, but not least, into various undercurrents apparent in life during the last forty years: movements taken all in all which, I feel sure, had certainly a greater influence on the outbreak of the World War than the wishes, personal feelings, and conscious actions of the leading men at the courts, in the chancelleries, and in the armies of the European Great Powers. But these are problems which lie outside the scope of these lectures.

CONCLUSION

IN my lectures I have sought to bring out the principal facts and events; to let the men who exercised an influence upon the course of those events speak for themselves, and then to leave it to my hearers and readers to pronounce judgement upon the aims and conduct of the British statesmen. I hope that at least one thing has been made clear; namely, that the men in control of British foreign policy held firmly to the basic principles which had (as I pointed out at the beginning of my lectures) inspired their predecessors for centuries in their policy towards the Continental Great Powers. It was quite obvious to British statesmen, during the decades that preceded the World War, that England must retain her supremacy at sea; that she could not permit any Continental Power to establish a hegemony in Europe and by so doing upset the European Balance of Power in a sense contrary to British interests; and finally, that she could not allow Belgium to pass into the hands of the strongest Continental Power. Since the *fear* that Germany entertained such plans increased from year to year, British statesmen held it to be their duty to make all possible preparations to be ready to defeat such plans if Germany should one day seek to put them into operation. Hence the increase in naval armaments, the successive agreements with their allies, and hence also their endeavours to win for England new friends. No British statesman desired the war; but many of them, and especially influential men in the Foreign Office, held it to be inevitable. Neither Lansdowne nor, later, Grey belonged to this school of thought. As we have seen, Grey made every endeavour to avoid a break with Germany. Whether or not the means he chose to effect his purpose were invariably the best is a question I cannot enter into here. What is indisputable, however, is that he acted in accordance with the traditional policy of

England when, at the outbreak of war between the Triple Alliance and the *Entente*, he brought England into the conflict on the side of the *Entente*. The war was decided in England's favour. Germany vanished from the number of England's possible rivals. But is the danger that England felt to be threatening her from Germany, finally, and from every side, overcome? Far be it from me to attempt to answer this question. For it least becomes the historian, who is a prophet with his eyes directed upon the past, to prophesy what the future holds. Nevertheless I cannot refrain at the end of these lectures from giving expression to my hope that in the future England's statesmen will take up the cause of European peace and civilization in friendly co-operation with other States for the benefit of England and for the good of mankind; that they will support the cause of peace among the nations and the promotion of common scientific progress; and that they will assist in restoring more and more that European culture to which England has contributed so greatly in past centuries.

BIBLIOGRAPHY

ASQUITH, H. H. *The Genesis of the War.* 1923.

BECKER, O. *Bismarcks Bündnispolitik.* 1923.
—— *Das französisch-russische Bündnis.* 1925.

BETHMANN-HOLLWEG, TH. V. *Betrachtungen zum Weltkrieg.* 2 vols. 1919–22.

BRANDENBURG, E. *Von Bismarck zum Weltkriege.* 1925. English ed. 1927.

British Documents on the Origins of the War 1898–1914. GOOCH and TEMPERLEY. 1927 ff.

BUCKLE, G. E. *The Life of Benjamin Disraeli*, vols. iv–vi.
—— *The Letters of Queen Victoria*, vols. v–vii.

CECIL, LADY GWENDOLEN. *Life of Robert A. T., Marquis of Salisbury*, vol. ii, 1921.

ECKARDSTEIN, H. *Lebenserinnerungen und politische Denkwürdigkeiten.* 3 Bde. 1919–21.

FAY, S. B. *The Origins of the World War*, vol. i. 1928.

FISCHER, E. *Holsteins Grosses Nein.* 1925.

FRIEDJUNG, H., PRIBRAM, A. F. *Das Zeitalter des Imperialismus 1884–1914.* 3 Bde. 1919 ff.

GOOCH, G. P. *History of Modern Europe 1878–1919.* 1st ed. 1923.

GREY, E., VISCOUNT OF FALLODON. *Twenty-five Years, 1892–1916.* 2 vols. 1925.

HALDANE, R. B., VISCOUNT. *Before the War.* 1920.

HALLER, J. *England und Deutschland um die Jahrhundertwende.* 1929.

HAMMANN, O. *Der neue Kurs.* 1918.
—— *Zur Vorgeschichte des Weltkriegs.* 1918.
—— *Der misverstandene Bismarck.* 1921.
—— *Deutsche Weltpolitik 1890–1912.* 1925.

HOHLFELD, H. E. J. *Geschichte des Deutschen Reiches 1871–1924.* 1924.

HOYOS GRAF, L. A. G. *Der deutsch-englische Gegensatz und sein Einfluss auf die Balkanpolitik Oesterreich-Ungarns.* 1922.

JAPIKSE, N. *Europa und Bismarcks Friedenspolitik.* 1927.

KÄBER, E. *Die Idee des europäischen Gleichgewichtes in der publizistischen Literatur des 16–18 Jh.* 1907.

KJELLÉN, R. *Die Grossmächte der Gegenwart 1917; neueste Auflage unter dem Titel 'Die Grossmächte vor und nach dem Weltkriege'.* 1930.
—— *Dreibund und Dreiverband.* 1921.

LEE, S. *Life of King Edward.* 2 vols. 1925–7.

LENZ, M. *Deutschland im Kreise der Grossmächte 1871–1914.* 1925.

LUTZ, H. *Lord Grey und der Weltkrieg.* 1927; English ed. 1928.

MARCKS, E. *Deutschland und England in den grossen europäischen Krisen seit der Reformation.* 1900.

MARCKS, E. *Die Einheitlichkeit der englischen Aussenpolitik von 1500 bis zur Gegenwart.* 1910.

MEINECKE, FL. *'Geschichte des deutsch-englischen Bündnisproblems 1898–1901.'* 1928. Ergänzung in *'Am Webstuhl der Zeit'*. *Erinnerungsgabe für H. Delbrück.*

NEWTON, LORD. *Lord Lansdowne.* 1929.

NICOLSON, H. *Sir Arthur Nicolson, 1849–1928: A Study in the Old Diplomacy.* 1930.

NOACK, U. *Bismarcks Friedenspolitik.* 1928.

Oesterreich-Ungarns Aussenpolitik, 1908–1914. 9 Bde. 1930.

Politik, die Grosse, der Europäischen Kabinette 1871–1917. 40 Bde. in 54 Bden. 1922–6.

PRELLER, H. *Salisbury und die türkische Frage im Jahre 1895.* 1930.

PRIBRAM, A. F. *Die politischen Geheimverträge Oesterreich-Ungarns.* 1920. English ed. 1920. French ed. 1923.

—— *Austrian Foreign Policy, 1908–1918.* 1923.

RACHFAHL, F. *Bismarcks Englische Bündnispolitik.* 1922.

RITTER, G. *Bismarcks Verhältnis zu England, und die Politik des Neuen Kurses.* 1924.

ROTHFELS, J. *Bismarcks Englische Bündnispolitik.* 1924.

TAUBE, H. *Fürst Bismarck zwischen Deutschland und England.* 1923.

TIRPITZ, A. *Pol. Dokumente.* 1927.

—— *Erinnerungen.* 1919.

WILHELM II. *Briefe an den Zaren, 1894–1914.* 1920. English ed.

INDEX OF PERSONS